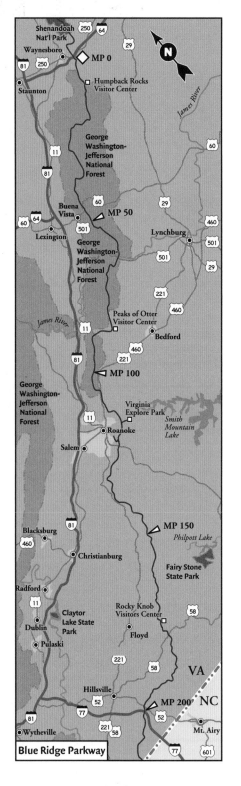
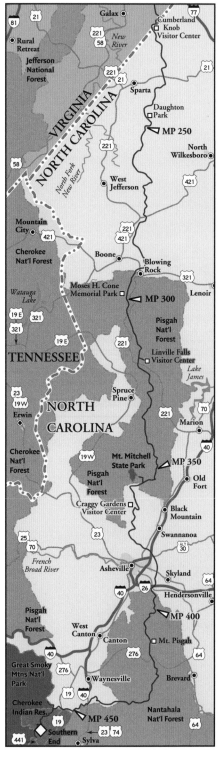

Blue Ridge Parkway

Third Edition

# Guide to the
# BLUE RIDGE PARKWAY

Victoria Logue

Frank Logue

Nicole Blouin

 Menasha Ridge Press
Birmingham, Alabama

Printed in China
Published by Menasha Ridge Press
Distributed by Publishers Group West
Third edition, first printing

Library of Congress Cataloging-in-Publication Data

Logue, Frank, 1963-
   Guide to the Blue Ridge Parkway / Frank Logue, Victoria Logue, Nicole
Blouin. -- 3rd ed.
   p. cm.
Includes index.
   ISBN-13: 978-0-89732-908-8
   ISBN-10: 0-89732-908-2
   1.  Blue Ridge Parkway (N.C. and Va.)--Guidebooks.  I. Logue,
Victoria, 1961- II. Blouin, Nicole, 1966- III. Title.

   F217.B6L56 2010
   917.5504'44--dc22

                                        2010017753


Cover and interior design by Grant Tatum
Cover photo © Jim Schemel
All photographs © 1997, 2003, 2010 by Frank Logue

Menasha Ridge Press
P.O. Box 43673
Birmingham, AL 35243
www.menasharidge.com

# Table of Contents

## Icon Key

Food

Information

Lodging

Picnic area

Campground

Trailhead

Tunnel

# Introduction

• • • • • • • • • • • • • • • • • • • • •

As your car leans around a bend in the Parkway lined with a bank of rhododendrons, yet another picture-perfect panoramic view opens up before you. Alternating between cool creeks shaded by oaks and pines to high mountain meadows with broad vistas, the Blue Ridge Parkway offers a visual delight at every turn. It is easy to imagine that this road was simply placed on a course through the already scenic Appalachian Mountains, but in reality, the Parkway is a much more ambitious project and the result of hard work on the part of a number of talented landscape architects and engineers. In December of 1933, Stanley W. Abbott, the first resident landscape architect and primary designer of the Blue Ridge Parkway, began working "with a ten-league canvas and a brush of a comet's tail," as he put it.

When Abbott first saw what he had to work with, he reported, "Few of the showplaces of the parkway environs remain in an unspoiled natural state." Planners faced land destroyed by clear cutting, cultivated farmland, and streams and rivers that ran brown due to erosion. Before the scenic beauty of the Parkway could be enjoyed, it had to be re-created, almost from scratch, as far as the bushes, trees, and lakes were concerned.

During that creation process, the 469-mile Parkway was designed to be a "drive awhile, stop awhile" recreation opportunity. To make this dream a reality, the route for the Parkway was carefully selected to emphasize scenic and historic areas. Scattered along its length were parks, historic sites, and other points of interest. Abbott referred to the roadway as the chain of a necklace, the parks and historic sites as bright jewels. For example, after leaving Cumberland Knob Visitor Center at the North Carolina–Virginia border, you will travel nearly 21 miles south, passing only overlooks and road crossings before reaching yet another jewel: Doughton Park. Each jewel offers a variety of recreational opportunities, including hiking trails, living-history demonstrations, interpretive information, picnic and camping facilities, and

**Mabry Mill**
**(MP 176.2)**

much more, creating a number of pleasant day drives along its route.

So pack a picnic basket, pile in the car, and come drive awhile, stop awhile.

## GEOLOGY AND GEOGRAPHY

From Shenandoah National Park in Virginia to the Great Smoky Mountains in western North Carolina, the Blue Ridge Parkway covers 469 miles—217 miles in Virginia, 252 in North Carolina. The Parkway begins at Rockfish Gap in Virginia, and for the next 355 miles, it leads south as it follows the Blue Ridge Mountains, the eastern bastion of the Appalachians. The Parkway leaves the Blue Ridge at Ridge Junction (milepost 355.3), skirting the southern edge of the Black Mountains before passing through the Great Craggy Range. From there, the Parkway descends to the valley of the French Broad River then climbs toward the summits of Pisgah Ledge and the Great Balsam Mountains en route to the Smokies.

*the Black Mountains and the nearby Balsam and Smoky mountains are home to 41 mountain peaks above 6,000 feet*

The Appalachian Mountains, through which the Parkway travels, were formed at the close of the Permian period more than 230 million years ago. At that time, the mountains towered more than 40,000 feet above sea level, more than 10,000 feet higher than Mount Everest. When the rocks were first formed in the Cambrian-Precambrian period (500 million to 1 billion years ago), they were laid down in a marine environment as thick beds of sedimentary rocks such as sandstone and shale. When the mountain uplift began at the end of the Permian age, heat and pressure transformed the sedimentary rocks into the metamorphic rocks—quartzite, schist, gneiss, marble, and slate—that you now see.

The Appalachians reveal an intricate series of folding and faulting as well as igneous intrusions. Vast sections of the mountains have undergone a minimum of three cycles of erosion to the level of peneplain, that is, reduced almost to a plain by erosion. Between each of these erosion cycles, the mountains were uplifted. This uplift is still occurring at the rate of about 1.5 inches every 1,000 years.

If you travel the entire Parkway from Rockfish Gap to the Oconaluftee River, you will traverse an area of diversified topography. From Rockfish Gap to Roanoke, Virginia, you will follow a master ridge with a number of spurs that bend parallel to the master ridge and often surpass it in height. To the east of this master ridge are the Piedmont lowlands; to the west, the Great Valley. On the other side of the Great Valley rise the Alleghenies.

From the Roanoke Valley south to where the Parkway leaves the Blue Ridge, you will pass through an extended plateau that unfolds to the west of the crest of the Blue Ridge. The rolling hills are the result of an uplifted peneplain. You will also see gently rounded knobs (monadnocks) dotting the landscape, prominent above the farmland. To the east, a steep slope plummets to the Piedmont. Here and there, finger ridges stretch as much as a mile into these lowlands.

Immense parallel ridges and their spurs are broken up by narrow valleys from the Black Mountains to the Smokies. Many summits rise to greater than 6,000 feet, a difference of more than 4,000 feet above the valleys.

North of the divide, from Rockfish Gap to the Roanoke Valley (milepost 0.0 to approximately milepost 105), water rising from springs in the Alleghenies forms creeks and rivers that flow across the route of the Parkway as the water makes its way to the Atlantic Ocean. The Blue Ridge Parkway follows 215 miles of the crest of the Blue Ridge Mountains from the Roanoke Valley to the Black Mountains. Along this eastern continental divide, water flows westward from the Blue Ridge toward the Gulf of Mexico and eastward toward the Atlantic Ocean. South of the Black Mountains (milepost 355.3), all water flows toward the Gulf of Mexico.

**“**

*the mountains of North Carolina and Tennessee were still considered wilderness in 1754*

**”**

## HISTORY OF THE AREA

The Appalachian Mountains have supported human life for thousands of years. Archaeological evidence from the Peaks of Otter area (milepost 86.0) indicates that a society of game hunters lived here more than 8,000 years ago. Artifacts from this period include spear tips, or Folsom points. This culture was succeeded by the more advanced mound-building society.

The more familiar Native American tribes eventually established power in the Blue Ridge. The Cherokee of North Carolina were the most powerful of the tribes that lived in the area through which the Parkway passes. The valleys of the Balsam and Smoky mountains were settled by the Cherokee. In Virginia, the Catawba tribe lived in the Catawba River Valley to the east of the Parkway. These two tribes fought continually with each other, as well as with the Iroquois, who often raided the territory south along the Great Valley.

By the beginning of the 18th century, the Iroquois had not only defeated the smaller Tupelo, Monoacan, and

Saponi tribes, but had nearly vanquished the Cherokee and Catawba as well. The Iroquois War Trail traversed the Blue Ridge area south to Big Lick (now Roanoke). Here, it forked westward and south through the Great Valley to the Tennessee River and its tributaries, which were occupied by the Cherokees, and eastward through the Blue Ridge, following the Roanoke River gap before heading south into the homeland of the Catawba. When European settlers arrived, they used these war trails as they began to settle the "wilderness."

From the 1730s until the beginning of the French and Indian War in 1754, settlers from Scotland, Ireland, England, and Germany used the Iroquois War Trail as they moved southward from Pennsylvania, settling western Virginia, western North Carolina, and eastern Tennessee. When the French and Indian War began, western Virginia was relatively settled. The mountains of North Carolina and Tennessee were still considered wilderness, and settlers fought not only the primitive conditions but also the Cherokee, who defended their territory until the end of the Revolutionary War.

The Cherokee were pushed back into the Great Smoky Mountains by settlers taking over their lands in the late 1700s. Disease and war took a heavy toll on the Cherokee, and by the 1830s, only about 20,000 members remained. Settlers pushed farther into the mountains of

**Johnson Farmhouse (MP 85.9)**

western North Carolina and northern Georgia, making confrontation unavoidable. An ironic twist to the fate of the Cherokee came during the War of 1812, in which General Andrew Jackson paved his path to fame and the presidency. The Cherokee, under the command of Junaluska, created a diversion that turned the tide of battle in Jackson's favor at the Battle of Horseshoe Bend in Alabama. Jackson went on to the presidency and in 1838 signed an agreement that called for the entire Cherokee nation to be moved to a reservation in Oklahoma. Under the direction of General Winfield Scott, 17,000 Cherokees were herded west at gunpoint. More than 4,000 of the Native Americans died on the forced march that became known as the Trail of Tears. In the Smokies, hundreds of Cherokee hid in the mountains. They later established what is now the Qualla Reservation at the southern end of the Parkway.

By the turn of the 19th century, the descendants of the Scots-Irish and other British settlers were the prevailing pioneers in the southern Appalachian Mountains. Daniel Boone, "Nolichucky Jack" Sevier, James Robertson, and Andrew Lewis are among the famous settlers and soldiers of the southern Appalachians.

From the beginning, the livelihood of the mountaineers was agriculture. Chief crops were corn, wheat, and potatoes. Most farmers also raised cattle and hogs, and a number owned sheep, geese, and turkey. The livestock and fowl were driven to market in the north and east each fall. With proceeds from the sale of animals, the farmers could purchase manufactured goods. This regional trade is just one sign that life along the Blue Ridge Mountains was not as isolated as the old mountaineer stereotypes would lead visitors to believe.

The people of the southern Appalachians were very nearly split on the subject of secession and the Civil War to which it led. In some cases, family fought against family. And as battles raged on distant fields, people living along the Blue Ridge were forced to contend with deserters, renegades, and raiders who sought the comparative safety of the mountains as a refuge.

Once the war ended in 1865, Blue Ridge farmers faced another threat to their families and lands as outside investors bought up mountain land for its timber and other natural resources. The farmers were only too glad to sell off the high ridges and other undesirable land the outsiders first wanted. In time, that loss of land created a need for farmers to find outside work to supplement their farm goods and income.

Narrow-gauge railroads climbed into the mountains, bringing with them the extractive logging and mining that offered seasonal jobs but depleted the natural resources of the Blue Ridge. Outside investors logged the prime timber in the early 1900s, leaving behind spent land and a radically changed lifestyle for the people living along the Blue Ridge.

In the aftermath of the Great Depression, government programs to stimulate America's depressed economy brought much-needed jobs and money to the Appalachians. This included the creation of national parks and national forests along the southern Appalachians.

## HISTORY OF THE BLUE RIDGE PARKWAY

The romantic notion of a road through the scenic southern Appalachian Mountains existed long before the Parkway's inception in the 1930s. Colonel J. H. Pratt, who worked for the North Carolina Geologic and Economic Survey, charted such a route prior to World War I. His proposed mountain road extended from Roanoke, Virginia, through North Carolina and on to Greenville, South Carolina. He was actually able to build a short section of his road in North Carolina before the war began. The current Parkway follows sections of the colonel's old road near Altapass, North Carolina (mileposts 323.0 to 326.0).

The idea that finally reached fruition occurred to several men nearly simultaneously. When President Franklin Delano Roosevelt toured the Civilian Conservation Corps (CCC) camps of Shenandoah National Park on August 11, 1933, he responded with enthusiasm to Virginia Senator Harry F. Byrd's recommendation that Skyline Drive be connected with a second scenic drive that would extend to the Great Smoky Mountains National Park.

In September, Byrd met with Virginia Governor G. J. Pollard and Theodore E. Straus of the Public Works Administration to discuss the possibility of a parkway. The governor approved the idea of the project and appointed Byrd chairman of a Virginia committee that would expedite the project.

In early October, Pollard sent letters to fellow governors J. C. B. Ehringhaus of North Carolina and Hill McAllister of Tennessee, inviting them to appoint similar committees. On October 17, a conference was held in Byrd's Washington, D.C., office with the state committees and others, including Senator R. R. Reynolds of North Carolina, National Park Service Director Arno B. Cammerer, and the chief of the Bureau of Public Roads, Thomas McDonald. The purpose of the meeting was "to consider ways and means of constructing a road to connect the two great national parks, Shenandoah National Park and Great Smoky Mountain National Park."

As everyone favored the road, a proposal was sent to Secretary of the Interior Harold L. Ickes, who also served as public works administrator. The proposal requested $16.6 million for a parkway whose route was as yet undecided.

Secretary Ickes informed Cammerer on November 18, 1933, that Roosevelt had approved the parkway on condition that Virginia, North Carolina, and Tennessee pay the cost of location surveys and acquire and deed the right-of-way to the United States. In December, $4 million was allocated for the highway to connect the Shenandoah and Great Smoky Mountains national parks. The project was then set up under the National Park Service and the Bureau of Public Roads. The participating states were requested to submit their proposals of planned routes to Secretary Ickes, and a hearing was scheduled for February of 1934.

At the hearing, the group ran into its first controversy— North Carolina and Tennessee proposed entirely different routes. Tennessee's route extended west from Linville, North Carolina, and continued south to the Great Smokies via the Unaka Mountains. North Carolina, on the other hand, wanted to continue the parkway south from Linville via the Blacks and the Balsams to enter the Smoky Mountains near Cherokee. Following a joint study by the National Park Service and the Bureau of Public Roads, which recommended the Tennessee route, Ickes approved only a route south from Shenandoah National Park to the James River and from Adney Gap, Virginia, to Blowing Rock, North Carolina, because of the outcry from North Carolina about the decision.

A second hearing was arranged, and in November Ickes announced that the parkway would run from Blowing Rock to the Great Smoky Mountains entirely in North Carolina. In the House of Representatives, there was a good deal of opposition to federal money being used to create a road whose only immediate benefit would be to Virginia and North Carolina. The act that finally made the parkway a reality narrowly passed the House then later cleared the Senate. On June 30, 1936, it was signed into law. It was in this act that the parkway was officially named the Blue Ridge Parkway. Prior to that, it had been called both the Appalachian Parkway and the Shenandoah to Great Smoky Mountains National Parkway.

As work on the Parkway progressed, those in charge met with little opposition. Like most of the country in the wake of the Depression, the Blue Ridge was economically depressed, and the idea of a paved road passing through this relatively undeveloped region appealed to many mountain residents. Acceptance was not universal, however, and resentment began to grow, with many of those who sold land for the Parkway angry that the road would bisect their farms. In most cases, ill will gradually changed to approval as Parkway neighbors grew to appreciate the road as an economic, recreational, and cultural resource.

## BUILDING THE PARKWAY

In 1933, the amount of work Parkway planners and builders faced was tremendous. Reconnaissance, surveying, the acquisition of rights-of-way, design and layout, the drawing up of specifications for contracts, letting and evaluating bids, supervising construction, landscaping, and final acceptance of each contract were just the beginning. Every item, no matter how small, had to pass through the gauntlet of approval, beginning in the field and often navigating all the way to the secretary of the interior before returning through the same route back to the field.

Landscape architect Stanley Abbott would later reminisce about the tremendous fieldwork needed to ensure that the Parkway was scenic and diverse, remarking that he and others would focus ". . . on the business of following a mountain stream for a while, then climbing upon the slope of a hill pasture, then dipping down into the open bottomlands and back into the woodlands."

But the Parkway was not to be built just to provide travelers with scenic views. The 1916 act that established the National Park Service stated that the road be built to "conserve the scenery and the natural and historic objects and the wildlife therein and to provide for the enjoyment of the same in such a manner and by such means as will leave them unimpaired for the enjoyment of future generations." Mabry Mill, Brinegar Cabin, and

*"*

*before Congress officially named it the Blue Ridge Parkway, the road was referred to as the Appalachian Parkway or the Shenandoah to Great Smoky Mountains National Parkway*

*"*

the Moses H. Cone Estate are among the architectural features that have become a part of the scenic route.

Preserving history and creating scenic landscapes were not all the landscape architects had in mind. A number of recreational parks and concession areas were also to be dispersed over the length of the Parkway. Funds were allocated and four areas were open by 1939, beginning with Cumberland Knob and followed by Smart View, Rocky Knob, and Doughton Park.

The first portion of the Parkway to be built was in the northernmost section of North Carolina—12.49 miles—with ground being broken in September of 1935. For the next 52 years, thousands of people worked to see the Parkway completed. In 1987, the last section—including the viaduct at Linn Cove—was finally opened to the public, completing a continuous road from Rockfish Gap in central Virginia to the Oconaluftee River near Cherokee, North Carolina.

The Parkway would have had to wait much longer for completion if it had not been for a number of donors. The Moses H. Cone Memorial Hospital of Greensboro, North Carolina, deeded 3,516 acres and a mansion to the Parkway in 1949 as the Moses H. Cone Memorial Park. The estate is partially supported by an annual donation of $10,000. That same year, the Jefferson Standard Life Insurance Company, also of Greensboro, North Carolina, deeded 3,900 acres as the Julian Price Memorial Park. In 1951, John D. Rockefeller, Jr., donated $95,000 so that the National Park Service and the U.S. Forest Service could purchase land in Linville Gorge. By April of 1952, 535 acres had been added to the Parkway to form the Linville Falls Recreation Area.

## PARKWAY SERVICES AND PARTNERS

Not all services could be provided by the National Park Service, so the secretary of the interior was authorized, through public law, to negotiate concession contracts. The first contracted concession was a bus service at Peaks of Otter. In 1950, Peaks of Otter, Inc., began transporting tourists to the summit of Sharp Top and providing lunch and souvenirs at the bus station. In 1958, Peaks of Otter, Inc., was replaced by the Virginia Peaks of Otter Company. By this time restaurant and service station facilities were available at Whetstone Ridge and Otter Creek. Since 1958, the company has built a 75-room lodge at Peaks of Otter that includes a restaurant. Authorized concessions are now

*the last portion of the Parkway was completed in 1987*

spaced at intervals along the length of the Parkway.

The National Park Service has created a variety of interpretive offerings for visitors driving along the Parkway. Visitor centers, self-guided trails, roadside signs, campfire programs, and guided nature walks are among the programs developed to provide visitors with information about the Parkway, its history, and its culture. Many of these programs are detailed in *Parkway Milepost,* a free, educational magazine found in visitor centers and other sites along the Parkway.

In addition, the National Park Service has developed partnerships with different organizations to help protect and preserve the culture and beauty associated with the Parkway. These organizations are noted in the brochure *Parkway Partners,* but of particular note is the Southern Highland Craft Guild. Located in the Parkway's Folk Art

View from Moses H. Cone
Memorial Park
(MP 294.0)

Center (milepost 382.0) near Asheville, North Carolina, the guild offers demonstrations, exhibits, and sales of traditional and contemporary arts and crafts.

The nine Parkway campgrounds are open from May to November. Between June 1 and Labor Day, campground stays are limited to 14 consecutive days and 30 total days per year in each campground. A fee is charged on a per-night basis, which includes up to two adults. An additional charge is collected for all other persons older than age 18. Children accompanied by an adult camp free. Drinking water, RV dump stations, and comfort stations are provided. None of the campgrounds are equipped with showers, electrical hookups, or laundry services. Campground quiet hours are from 10 p.m. to 6 a.m. Winter camping is occasionally available, weather permitting. Inquire in advance, as facilities are limited. Reservations are accepted at some campgrounds. Tent sites are almost always available, but RV sites can fill up in peak season, particularly on weekends. Two nice, but lesser used, campgrounds are Roanoke Mountain in Virginia and Crabtree Meadows in North Carolina. Most campgrounds have wheelchair-accessible facilities.

| Mile | Campground | Tents | RVs | Elev. (ft.) |
| --- | --- | --- | --- | --- |
| 60.9 | Otter Creek | 45 | 24 | 800 |
| 85.9 | Peaks of Otter | 82 | 59 | 2,565 |
| 120.4 | Roanoke Mountain | 74 | 30 | 1,500 |
| 167.1 | Rocky Knob | 81 | 28 | 3,100 |
| 239.2 | Doughton Park | 110 | 25 | 3,600 |
| 296.9 | Julian Price | 129 | 68 | 3,400 |
| 316.4 | Linville Falls | 50 | 20 | 3,000 |
| 339.5 | Crabtree Meadows | 71 | 22 | 3,750 |
| 408.8 | Mount Pisgah | 70 | 70 | 5,000 |

## LODGING AND DINING

Lodges operated by concessionaires are at Peaks of Otter, Doughton Park, and Mount Pisgah, and housekeeping cabins are available at Rocky Knob. Most of the six restaurants on the Parkway are open from mid-April until November 1, though the Peaks of Otter lodge and restaurant are operated year-round. Restaurants are located at the following mileposts:

60.8   Otter Creek
85.9   Peaks of Otter
176.2  Mabry Mill
241.1  Doughton Park
339.5  Crabtree Meadows
408.6  Mount Pisgah

## BICYCLING

The Parkway challenges bicyclists with more than 48,000 vertical feet to climb, whether you bike the 469 miles northbound or southbound. The Parkway was designed as a driving road and does not have broad shoulders for bikers. Select clothing that is highly visible, wear a helmet, equip your bike with reflectors, and avoid riding in dense fog. Lights are required to bike through the tunnels on the Parkway.

The National Park Service has a flyer on biking the Parkway that lists the major climbs and shows elevation changes between mileposts. Bikes are allowed only on the Parkway, in campgrounds, and in parking areas. No bikes are permitted on Parkway trails.

## HIKING

Trails along the Parkway range from short leg stretchers to a portion of the 2,100-mile Appalachian Trail. Many of the trails are listed in this book. Campgrounds and visitor

Sunrise view from Fox Hunters Paradise Trail (MP 218.6)

centers provide free maps of trails in their area. A list of trailheads by milepost can be found in Appendix C of this book or at visitor centers along the Parkway. Good hiking shoes and water are recommended for trails more than a mile in length.

For hikes longer than a leg stretcher, you will want to let someone know where you will be hiking and what time you expect to return. That will speed efforts to assist you in an emergency.

### FISHING

Bring your rod and lure hat with you to the Parkway. The Parkway offers more than a hundred miles of game-fish streams and 13 lakes, which range in size from a city lot to the 47-acre Price Lake (milepost 296.7).

The rivers and small streams at lower elevations support the native resident game fish of the Southern Highlands—the brook trout. Some streams and Parkway lakes have been stocked with nonnatives such as rainbow trout from the mountains of the West and brown trout from Europe. The larger waterways, including the French Broad, Linville, Roanoke, Swannanoa, and James rivers, support their own mix of native and introduced fish, plus warm-water residents such as bass.

A fishing license from North Carolina or Virginia is required for fishing along the Parkway. No special trout license is required to fish Parkway waters. Season, hours, creel, and size limits are all determined by state laws. No fishing is allowed in Parkway waters from one-half hour after sunset until one-half hour before sunrise. Streams and lakes labeled special waters have additional regulations.

The dam at Price Lake, the footbridge in the Price Lake picnic area, and the James River Bridge are off-limits to fishing. Because of research efforts, Bee Tree Creek, a tributary of Boone Fork, is closed to fishing.

For more information about fishing on the Parkway, as well as the types of game fish found in specific creeks and lakes, ask for a copy of *Fishing Regulations and Opportunities* available at most visitor centers.

### SWIMMING

No swimming is allowed in Parkway waters. However, some nearby public lakes have swimming areas.

### DISABLED ACCESS

Most of the Parkway's visitor centers, contact stations, restaurants, and other facilities are wheelchair-accessible. In addition, there are three wheelchair-accessible trails. The trail to view the Linn Cove Viaduct (milepost 304.0) is a broad paved path. The paved trail at Mabry Mill (milepost 176.2) is wheelchair-accessible for all but the section that goes over the millrace on wooden steps. The famous view of the mill and millpond can be accessed from the main parking area. The mill itself and the other exhibits along the trail are accessed from the overflow parking area at milepost 175.9. And at Price Lake (milepost 296.9), a short wheelchair-accessible trail to a dock affords a pleasant view over the water.

For more information on disabled access at specific facilities, call (828) 271-4779.

## RANGER TALKS AND WALKS

The park service interprets its unique natural environment for visitors through literature, self-guided trails, scenic overlooks, exhibits, and informative signs. The idea, of course, is to encourage the traveler to stop awhile and learn more about the nature and culture of the Blue Ridge.

As an integral part of this interpretive program, the Parkway sponsors a variety of nature and history talks and walks from June through October at many areas along the motor road. These scheduled programs are usually led by park rangers and volunteers.

Activities include campfire circles and guided nature walks, as well as slide shows, musical demonstrations, and history talks. Offerings vary from one area to another.

Talks and walks are usually planned for weekend evenings just about sunset, with occasional programs on weekdays. Most programs are held at the amphitheaters along the Parkway. All ranger talks and walks, as well as most special events, are free, though there is a fee for some special events. Schedules are posted at visitor centers, concession areas, and campground entrances.

## DRIVING SAFETY

Because the Parkway is managed for recreation, travel is limited to passenger vehicles including motorcycles, cars, vans, pickup trucks, RVs, and tour buses. No commercial traffic is allowed. Unless otherwise posted, the speed limit is 45 mph. An average speed of 30 mph is helpful to estimate driving times along the Parkway, though speeds will be much lower in fog or rain.

Use extra caution in rain, fog, and snow, and be aware of wildlife. Deer and other animals may bolt in front of your car. Tunnels are potentially dangerous; slow down, use your headlights, and watch for cyclists. Place valuables in the trunk when a vehicle is left unattended, and contact the local ranger station or visitor center if a vehicle will be left overnight.

Parking is not limited to overlooks. Unless you find a "no parking" sign, feel free to stop anywhere along the shoulder of the Parkway where you find safe visibility and adequate space. Pull your car completely off the motor road, about 6 to 12 feet from the pavement.

## RULES AND REGULATIONS

The following are a few of the regulations which Parkway visitors need to be aware of:

- Pets must be on a leash no longer than six feet or under physical control (caged or carried).
- Harming animals and harvesting plants and natural features (such as rocks) are strictly prohibited.
- Historic or natural objects are not to be damaged or removed from the Parkway.
- Weapons are prohibited except when unloaded, packed, and stored in vehicles.
- Open containers of alcoholic beverages are permitted only in campgrounds by registered guests, and at picnic areas while picnicking, with no open containers allowed after 9 p.m.
- Camp only in designated areas.
- Stay on designated trails.
- Fires are prohibited except in campgrounds, at picnic areas, and at backcountry campsites by permit. Fires must be confined to fireplaces and grills.
- Park lakes and ponds are for scenic beauty and fishing enjoyment only, not for swimming, wading, or ice skating.
- Viewing wildlife at night with artificial lights is prohibited.

Park Watch encourages visitors to get involved in the protection and preservation of the Parkway. While traveling the Parkway, visitors should be alert to fire, crime, theft, safety hazards, and traffic problems, as well as violations of Parkway rules and regulations. Report to a park employee by calling (800) PARK-WATCH (727-5928).

## THE FOUR SEASONS OF THE PARKWAY

The personality of the Parkway changes with every season. Colors shift from pastels and greens to autumn shades and earth tones. As the months fall off the calendar, foliage blooms and flourishes and withers away. The weather turns from mild to warm, from cool to cold. Special events along the Parkway reflect the season; for example, in October you can often watch apple butter, and occasionally sorghum, being made at Mabry Mill.

Spring begins on the Parkway by late March, with an occasional snowstorm to surprise the lowlander. Creeks and rivers overflow from April rains, which bring out wildflowers to blanket the earth. All visitor centers and concession areas open in May.

Summer brings the busiest season on the Parkway and the best time to catch interpretive programs and special events. The pink-and-purple procession of flowering rhododendrons peaks around the first two weeks of June, with some varieties blooming into July; flowers bloom along the roadside all summer. While temperatures are usually mild, the dog days of August may send you in search of the Parkway's higher elevations, which rarely reach temperatures above 80°.

Autumn delivers a brilliant display of red, yellow, and orange as the leaves begin to turn—an excellent time for a drive along the motor road. Leaf peepers begin to enjoy the Parkway in late September. The peak for much of the Parkway falls around the second and third week of October, though this varies by tree species and elevation. The foliage starts changing colors at higher elevations, then flows down the mountains as October days pass. Though leaf season is popular on the Parkway, traffic is lighter during the week than on the weekend.

Winter is a wonderful time to find solitude on the Parkway. Formations of ice create picturesque sculptures on roadside cliffs, and the snow-covered ground brings a stillness to the forest. Bare trees open up incredible views, beauty in a colorless scene—white on gray and brown. Sections of the Parkway close throughout the winter depending on the weather. Even if it isn't snowing, the Parkway may be closed due to ice buildup or storm damage. These sections are often open to hikers, sledders, and cross-country skiers, so enjoy. Call (704) 298-0398, the Parkway's information number (tape recording), for a list of closings.

(On following page)
Abbott Lake at Peaks of
Otter Lodge
(MP 85.6)

# A Blue Ridge Sampler

• • • • • • • • • • • • • • • • • • • • •

Driving south from Rockfish Gap presents visitors with a quick introduction to the natural, cultural, and recreational resources the Blue Ridge Parkway has to offer.

During the first 63 miles, these resources are closely linked to transportation. A remnant of animal-drawn transportation is encountered at milepost 5.8, where a trace of the Old Howardsville Turnpike can be reached from a trail to the east of the Parkway. Humpback Rocks, south of the Humpback Rocks Visitor Center, is a landmark on the turnpike that stands watch over the Parkway. When the area along the Parkway was explored and later settled by Europeans, draft-drawn carts were the only means of getting into these mountains. During that period, Rockfish Gap (milepost 0.0) was an important route between the Rockfish and Shenandoah valleys.

Farther south you find the restored James River and Kanawha Canal Lock No. 7 (milepost 63.6). This was one of 90 locks built to move boats up the James River from Richmond to Buchanan in the 1800s. River travel was an important link to the mountains for a time, but it was soon eclipsed by the railroads.

Today, railroad tracks operate at each end of this

63-mile section. At milepost 0.0 in Rockfish Gap, the Chesapeake & Ohio Railroad passes under the gap in a tunnel. The remnant of a logging railroad at Yankee Horse Ridge (milepost 34.4) shows one of the major forces for change along the Blue Ridge. With the coming of the railroad, the building boom taking place along the East Coast gained access to two important natural resources of the mountains—coal and lumber—and consequently a third, manpower. The tracks along the James River use the same path once taken by the James River and Kanawha Canal (milepost 63.6) for some of its route.

Recreational resources of the Parkway are not limited to parking overlooks—numerous trails offer everything from leg stretchers to the 2,100-mile Appalachian Trail. The area around Peaks of Otter has been a place of respite and recreation since the 18th century. Before that time, Native Americans—Algonquin, Sioux, Iroquois, and

Fog rolls over Otter Lake
(MP 63.1)

Cherokee—used this area as a hunting and camping ground as they followed the well-worn elk, buffalo, and deer trails across the ridges. Archaeological evidence indicates that more than 8,000 years ago, prehistoric people found wildlife plentiful in the Peaks area.

The first "hotel" in this former farming community was Polly Wood's Ordinary, an inn that furnished simple lodging and meals for travelers from 1834 until 1860.

A few years before Polly Wood's inn closed, another hotel was built. Hotel Mons was constructed in 1857. It burned in 1870 but was soon rebuilt and continued to accommodate 40 guests and staff until 1936. The building was dismantled in the early 1940s.

> **"** *archaeological evidence indicates that prehistoric people lived in this area more than 8,000 years ago* **"**

The Peaks community was established in 1766 when Thomas Wood settled in the cabin on what is now known as Johnson Farm. Wood passed the farming tradition from generation to generation until 1852, when the Johnson family bought the original four-room cabin from James Joplin, a Wood descendant. Until Polly Wood's Ordinary opened in 1834, local homeowners would occasionally take in guests. The Johnsons were very much involved with the communities of Mons and the Peaks, and they (and the Bryants who succeeded them) often took overflow guests from Hotel Mons. The Bryants lived at Johnson Farm through the 1930s, when the area was purchased by the National Park Service. At that time, more than 20 families lived in the Peaks area.

A nearly 30-year break in the lodging tradition occurred during Parkway construction, but the tradition resumed with the opening of Peaks of Otter Lodge in 1964.

Another interesting fact about this section of the Parkway is that it features the lowest point on the Parkway and the highest Parkway elevation in Virginia. This section reaches its lowest elevation at the James River at 649 feet and climbs back up into the Blue Ridge, reaching 3,950 feet on Apple Orchard Mountain at milepost 76.7.

At Rockfish Gap, the towns of Waynesboro and Staunton, Virginia, are west on US 250. In Staunton, the Museum of Frontier Culture interprets the agricultural traditions of the area. East of Rockfish Gap is Charlottesville, Virginia, with the University of Virginia; President Thomas Jefferson's home, Monticello; and other attractions.

At milepost 45.6, Buena Vista and Lexington, Virginia, are west of the Parkway. Lexington's historic downtown is closely linked to the Civil War, a heritage highlighted at Washington and Lee University, the Stonewall Jackson

House, and other attractions.

At milepost 63.6, Lynchburg, Virginia, is east of the Parkway. Lynchburg's City Market, Bateau Landing, and museums are popular attractions. The Lynchburg Visitor Center is located at 216 East 12th Street and offers regional travel information.

## 0.0

### Rockfish Gap—I-64 and US 250

This gap has long been an important route between the Rockfish and Shenandoah valleys. Construction of the Crozet Tunnel, as it was called, began in 1858. After eight years of work, without the benefit of dynamite or heavy machinery, the two ends of the tunnel met 510 feet beneath the gap. Confederate General "Stonewall" Jackson marched his troops through the tunnel to join Confederate forces in Staunton during the Civil War. Today, the C&O Railroad line passes through the gap in a tunnel, and the gap is dominated by the highways.

Rockfish Gap was often mentioned on the popular 1970s television show *The Waltons*. The fictional family lived nearby and would occasionally travel through the gap. Author Earl Hamner, Jr., whose writings were the inspiration for the series, grew up in this area.

Today, this gap provides good opportunities to watch for hawks during their migration.

A chamber of commerce information center at the gap features a relief map of the area and information on the Blue Ridge Parkway, Skyline Drive, and surrounding attractions. US 250 leads 4.5 miles west to Waynesboro, and I-64 leads 21 miles east to Charlottesville.

## 0.2

### Afton Overlook

Rockfish Tavern, once located near this overlook, was a popular stagecoach stop. Thomas Jefferson, James Madison, and others met here in 1818 to select Charlottesville as the location for the University of Virginia. The town of Afton is 1,100 feet below in the valley.

## 1.5

### Rockfish Valley Overlook

This river valley was home to the Tuscarora tribe in the 1700s. Following their defeat by settlers on the Carolina coast, they moved northward, settling here. They later pushed farther north and became the sixth nation in the Iroquois Confederation.

> "
> *Rockfish Gap has long been an important route between the Rockfish and Shenandoah valleys*
> "

## 2.9
### View Shenandoah Valley

During the winter, you can see the immense lands of Beverly Manor from this viewpoint. This land was part of a Great Valley land grant given by the colonial government of Virginia. The 118,000 acres of the manor were settled by Scots-Irish immigrants.

## 5.8
### Humpback Rocks Visitor Center

The stone visitor center (open May through October) houses restrooms, an information desk, rural life exhibits, and an interpretive area focused on the area's pioneer life and outdoor recreation features.

The Mountain Farm Museum is the highlight of this stop. Outside, several preserved buildings are located on the path that leads south from the visitor center. This

An 1890 cabin at Humpback Rocks Visitor Center (MP 5.8)

Many large mammals have disappeared from the southern Appalachians, including the woodland buffalo, the wolf, and the mountain lion. The last American elk, also known as wapiti, was shot in 1855. Traces of these great mammals, often weighing as much as 1,000 pounds, can still be found in place names. Elk Valley, Banner Elk, and Elk Park are just a few of the places named in honor of this animal.

In 1917, with the buffalo, elk, mountain lion, and wolf gone, and the deer, bobcat, and bear quickly disappearing, elk were reintroduced to their former habitat. That year, more than 100 elk were transported from Yellowstone National Park

area was once known as the William J. Carter Farm, after the man who bought a farm in the late 1800s for $3 per acre with Confederate money. The Carter Farm buildings have long since disappeared, but Parkway planners moved period buildings in from other areas and arranged them on the site for this mountain farm exhibit. The 0.25-mile trail leads past a cabin, weasel-proof chicken coop, root cellar, barn with bear-proof hogpen, and springhouse. The cabin was built in 1890 by Billy and Nannie Ramsey at milepost 51.4 of the Parkway, and they used the cabin for the next 30 years. On summer weekends, rangers in period clothing are at the farm to give demonstrations and answer questions. This outdoor exhibit is wheelchair-accessible.

The Humpback Rocks Visitor Center is named for the prominent rock outcrop just south on the Parkway. The rocks were used as a landmark to guide teamsters carrying goods over the mountains on the Old Howardsville Turnpike. The turnpike was a major trade route in the mid-1800s and remained in use until the railroad came in 1880. The trace is still visible across the Parkway to the southeast of the visitor center parking lot.

**"**

*the rocks at Humpback Rocks were an important landmark to early settlers*

**"**

### 6.0

**Humpback Gap Overlook**

An interpretive sign in the parking area describes how early settlers cleared trees to make room for farmlands in the mountains. Settlers girdled the trees to kill them, then planted their first crops of corn among the dying trees to get crops going as soon as possible.

The Appalachian Trail passes through this overlook. Go south 0.9 miles on the A.T. to Humpback Rocks. It is a tough climb to a rewarding view.

and released in several locations in Virginia. In the Peaks of Otter area, 25 elk were reestablished. In 1935, more elk were brought to Peaks of Otter, and at one point the area boasted a population of 85 elk.

Unfortunately, times had changed. The lower elevations (the elks' winter habitat) blanketed with timber were formerly apple orchards. Farmers, finding the marauding elk in their orchards, shot them on the spot. The elk were also attacked by a brain parasite, common to the white-tailed deer but fatal to the elk. By 1971 the elk had once again disappeared from Virginia.

## 8.5

### Humpback Rocks Picnic Area

Picnic tables, as well as water fountains and restrooms, are scattered among the trees in this wooded area.

## 8.8

### Greenstone Overlook

The 0.2-mile Greenstone Trail leads to an example of the volcanic rocks that metamorphosed to form the dominant geologic feature at the northern end of the Blue Ridge Parkway. The catoctin greenstone gets its name from the distinctive green tint of the old lava flows. Enjoy fine views from this self-guiding trail, which interprets the geologic formations by way of small metal signs along the path. You can also see remnants of "hog walls" built in the 1800s.

## 9.6

### Dripping Rock Parking Area

In this introductory section of the Parkway, Dripping Rock parking area points out the diversity that Parkway planners had in mind as they created the Parkway. Unlike the big views you often see at overlooks, Dripping Rock is in a wooded setting. Though many parking areas offer long-range views, expect the occasional counterpoint such as this one in a forest and fern-filled setting. The white blazes on the trees mark the path of the Appalachian Trail through here.

## 10.4

### Rock Point Overlook

Catoctin greenstone can be seen just below this overlook.

As you drive along the length of the Parkway, you will notice that thousands of acres alongside the scenic route are farmed, growing a variety of traditional crops, including tobacco, cabbage, and other produce. When the Parkway was designed, planners created a route providing visual variety for those touring its length. As the planned route passed through many existing farms, the park service developed a program to allow farmers to lease portions of the right-of-way to continue to farm it. Not only did this program allow farming to continue, but it also maintained the original agricultural character of many areas of the Parkway and reduced maintenance costs.

### 10.7
### Raven's Roost Parking Overlook
The broad rock ledge at this overlook is an ideal roosting site for ravens and a popular location for hang gliding and rock climbing. (A permit is required for hang gliding.)

### 11.7
### Hickory Spring Parking Area
Hickory trees provided settlers with hardwood for tool handles. Hickory lends a distinctive flavor to smoked meat.

### 13.1
### Three Ridges Mountain
The high point (3,900 feet) on Three Ridges is 3 miles south.

### 13.7
### Reeds Gap—VA 664
The Appalachian Trail passes through the dirt parking area in Reeds Gap on the east side of the Parkway. This gap sits at the head of Reeds Creek.

### 15.4
### Love Gap
This gap is named for the Love, Virginia, post office, which was located nearby until 1944. The post office itself was named for Lovey Coffey, the daughter of the first postmaster at this office. The post office's name made it a popular stop each February with people mailing Valentine's Day cards.

### 16.0
### VA 814
Sherando Lake Recreation Area in the George Washington National Forest is 4.5 miles west of the Parkway on VA 814. The park has a 22-acre lake for swimming, boating, and fishing and a 7-acre lake that is limited to

The land is granted to farmers under special-use permits. Farmers are required to follow the stipulated good land-use practices, which include crop rotation, erosion control, and limited grazing (they must follow rules in accordance with the carrying capacity of the land). The farmers own everything they produce.

The National Park Service also purchased scenic easements on the land to promote traditional land uses along the Parkway. While a scenic easement does restrict uses of the land to agriculture and other compatible uses, ownership stays with the original owners.

fishing. The tent and RV campsites here, unlike those on the Parkway, have hot showers in the bathhouse. For more information, contact the Pedlar Ranger District at (540) 291-2188.

## 17.6

### The Priest
The 0.2-mile Priest Overlook Trail leads to a bench with a view of Priest Mountain, which is part of the Religious Range just east of the Parkway. Other peaks in the range include The Friar, The Cardinal, and Little Priest. The Priest was named for the de Priest family, who were early settlers in this area. This overlook offers an exhibit on hickory trees.

## 18.5

### White Rock Gap
An unmarked dirt parking area is on the west side of the Parkway. On the opposite side, you will find the trailhead for White Rock Falls Trail. From here go 1.6 miles to the falls, and another 0.9 miles to the other trailhead on the east side of the Parkway just north of Slacks Overlook (milepost 19.9).

## 19.0

### 20 Minute Cliff
This landmark's name comes from farmers in the valley below who said that during the June and July corn-chopping season, they could watch the sun on this cliff to know when they had 20 minutes until sunset.

## 19.9

### The Slacks Overlook
White Rock Falls Trail, just north of the parking area on the east side of the Parkway, leads 0.9 miles to the falls, 2.5 miles to White Rock Gap, and 4.5 miles to

Sherando Campground in the George Washington National Forest.

### 22.1
### Bald Mountain Parking Area
This is not a southern bald like those found on the Parkway in North Carolina. Here, there is no mystery as to why trees had trouble growing on the rocky mountain soil. Time and weathering have given the mountain more trees than when it was first named.

### 23.0
### Fork Mountain Overlook
Fork Mountain can be seen between the north and south forks of the Tye River.

**White Rock Falls**
**(MP 19.9)**

## 26.4

### Big Spy Overlook

The 0.1-mile Big Spy Trail leads up a gentle grassy hill to a view of the Shenandoah Valley and loops back to the parking area. Big Spy and nearby Little Spy served as lookout posts for Union sympathizers during the Civil War.

## 27.2

### Tye River Gap—VA 56

Drive 0.75 miles east to Montebello and 6.5 miles west to the town of Steele's Tavern, where Cyrus McCormick demonstrated the first mechanical reaper in 1831. The invention revolutionized agriculture by reducing the number of laborers required to harvest crops.

## 29.0

### Whetstone Ridge Visitor Center

This area was once known for its fine-grained sandstone used to make sharpening stones. District office with public restrooms, parking area, and picnic tables. Access the 12-mile Whetstone Ridge Trail here.

## 31.4

### Stillhouse Hollow Parking Area

This hollow was named not for an illegal moonshine still, but for a tax-paying apple stillhouse, or distillery, that made legal liquor before Prohibition came with the 18th Amendment to the Constitution in 1919.

## 34.4

### Yankee Horse Ridge Parking Area

A 200-foot section of the Irish Creek Railway, including a low trestle, can be seen at this overlook. This narrow-gauge rail line was originally built by the South River Lumber Company to gain access to stands of trees that had been left virtually untouched until the turn of the 20th century. The railbed has been preserved, but the tracks seen today are a reconstruction of a 50-mile line built in 1919 and completed in 1920. This track carried more than 100 million board feet of lumber to the mill. The last timber-cutting in the area was near Crabtree Falls in 1938, after which the region was logged out.

The 0.2-mile Yankee Horse Trail leads from this overlook to 30-foot Wigwam Falls and loops back to the parking area. The falls get their name from Wigwam Mountain, where local tradition says a Native American hunting camp was once located.

### 37.4
### Irish Gap

As the place names along this section attest, many of the region's settlers came from Ireland. Irish immigrants played an important role in the construction of the James River and Kanawha Canal (milepost 63.6). A common adage of the day stated that all you needed to build a canal was "a pick, a shovel, a wheelbarrow, and an Irishman."

### 38.8 
### Boston Knob Overlook

The 0.1-mile Boston Knob Loop Trail offers you a chance to stretch your legs. The trail is surrounded by dogwood trees and wild azaleas that bloom in spring. A picnic table is located here.

### 40.0
### Clarks Gap

The gap is named for the Clark family, who received a land grant for service in the War of 1812.

### 43.0
### Irish Creek Valley Overlook

Also named for the Irish immigrants to this area, Irish Creek is a local white-water rafting and kayaking spot.

### 44.4
### Whites Gap Overlook

Jordan Toll Road crossed the Blue Ridge near this overlook. This stage route was an important traverse point on this ridge south of Rockfish Gap.

### 44.9
### Chimney Rock Mountain Overlook

View of Chimney Rock Mountain, one of many geologic formations on the Parkway named for its appearance.

### 45.6
### Humphries Gap—US 60

Four miles west to Buena Vista; 11 miles west to Lexington; 22 miles east to Amherst. This is a good spot to watch the annual hawk migration.

### 45.7
### View Buena Vista

Buena Vista, Virginia, lies 1,500 feet below the Parkway. In 1847, the Battle of Buena Vista in the Mexican-American War was fought with weaponry made from iron forged in the town, then known as Green Valley. The town's name was changed to herald its connection to the successful assault.

## 47.5
### Indian Gap Parking Area
The 0.2-mile Indian Gap Trail is a loop leading to an interesting group of truck-sized boulders.

## 48.9
### Licklog Spring Gap
The name *licklog* is used to identify several gaps and other geographic features along the Parkway. It referred to an area where farmers would rub salt into a notch in a downed log to give their livestock that ranged in the mountains a source of the salt they needed in their diets.

## 49.4
### View House Mountain
Across the Great Valley, Big House and Little House mountains can be seen in the Alleghenies and make up the 950-acre House Mountain Preserve.

## 50.5
### Robinson Gap
This gap is named for John Robinson, an Irish immigrant who fought in the American Revolution.

## 51.5
### Unmarked Parking Area
The Appalachian Trail crosses the Parkway at this small parking area.

## 52.8
### Bluff Mountain Overlook
An interpretive sign at this overlook describes the George Washington National Forest, the largest national forest in the East. It is now adminstered jointly with the Jefferson National Forest.

The ghost of Ottie Cline Powell reportedly haunts the summit of Bluff Mountain. In the fall of 1890, four-year-old Ottie went into the woods to gather firewood for his schoolhouse and never returned. Extensive searches didn't turn up the boy's body. It was found five months later well away from the school, on top of Bluff Mountain.

## 53.1
### Bluff Mountain Tunnel
This 630-foot tunnel is the northernmost tunnel on the Parkway and the only one in Virginia.

*"*

*George Washington supported building a canal system along the James and Potomac rivers*

*"*

The Blue Ridge Parkway is a linear national park that passes through several national forests. So what's the difference between the two? National parks primarily provide for preservation and are under the U.S. Department of the Interior. The National Park Service interprets the natural, historical, and cultural significance of its parks and provides myriad recreational opportunities. The U.S. Forest Service, which manages the national forests, is under the U.S. Department of Agriculture and is charged with administering the country's timberland. While national forests also provide a host of recreational opportunities, their multiuse ethic is geared toward a working forest, where trees are grown and harvested for timber.

For more than 180 miles of the Parkway's length, the scenic route passes through the George Washington and Jefferson national forests in Virginia and the Pisgah and Nantahala national forests in North Carolina.

**"** *panther, painter, catamount, and cougar are all names used for the mountain lion (Felix concolor)* **"**

### 53.6
### View Rice Mountain
Wooded views with picnic table.

### 55.1
### White Oak Flats Overlook
The 0.1-mile White Oak Flats Trail offers a chance to walk alongside a small stream.

### 55.8
### Dancing Creek Overlook
This parking area is situated on the banks of a creek with a table available for picnicking.

### 57.6
### Upper Otter Creek Overlook
Naturalists often hear that water moccasins are seen on Otter Creek, but it is usually the northern water snake that visitors see. It is a dark-colored nonvenomous snake that will readily bite if cornered.

### 58.2
### Otter Creek Flats Overlook
The unique two-bay design of this overlook is charming and unusual. Picnic tables are situated on the banks of the creek, although the shallow banks, or flats, are prone to flooding in heavy rain.

## 59.7
### Otter Creek Overlook

Several unconfirmed sightings of mountain lions have occurred in the Otter Creek area in recent years. The big cats were previously believed to have disappeared from this area in the 19th century. Mountain lions are sometimes reported by visitors to the Blue Ridge, but the feline's return remains unconfirmed.

## 60.4
### The Riffles Overlook

This parking area is at a 20-foot, chutelike cascade on Otter Creek.

## 60.8
### Otter Creek

The Otter Creek area has a lot to offer Parkway visitors. The area has a campground with 45 tent and 24 trailer sites, restrooms, water, and a campfire circle. Many of the campsites are along the banks of Otter Creek. A restaurant, gift shop, and restrooms are also at the parking area by the Parkway.

The 3.5-mile Otter Creek Trail follows the creek down to the James River Visitor Center. The trail can also be accessed from the next three overlooks to the south.

## 61.4
### Terrapin Hill Overlook—VA 130

This overlook offers access to Otter Creek Trail and a picnic table.

## 62.5
### Lower Otter Creek Overlook

In April, the area from here to the James River is one of the best places on the Parkway to see the pink flowers of redbud trees in bloom. Bridges over Otter Creek offer access to Otter Creek Trail. Picnic tables are also available in this picturesque spot.

## 63.1
### Otter Lake

Two parking areas are located alongside the lake. The larger area is the northernmost. It is alongside the middle of the lake, which parallels the Parkway. The smaller lot is at Otter Lake Dam. From either parking area, you can follow the 0.8-mile Otter Lake Loop Trail that follows the shore of the lake and crosses Otter Creek Trail twice.

Whether by themselves or in small herds, deer are often seen grazing in fields along the Parkway. The proliferation of deer in the Blue Ridge is amazing when you consider that the species had nearly disappeared from these mountains at the turn of the 20th century. Farming and logging had taken away the white-tailed deer's forest habitat, while hunting severely diminished the numbers of those remaining.

With the purchase of national park and national and state forest

### 63.2
### Lowest Elevation on the Parkway
At 649.4 feet, this spot is the lowest elevation on the Parkway. From here the Parkway will climb more than 3,300 feet in the next 13.5 miles to the highest point on the Parkway in Virginia, at Apple Orchard Mountain.

The highest point overall on the Parkway is on Richland Balsam (elevation 6,047 feet) in North Carolina, at milepost 431.4.

### 63.6
### James River Visitor Center

**James River and Kanawha Canal (MP 63.6)**

This visitor center is located at the James River Water Gap. This gap through the Blue Ridge was carved by the awesome force of the water cutting away at the rocks over time. The bridge over the James was opened in 1965.

lands, both federal and state governments began to rebuild the forests of the Appalachians and once again provide the deer with the habitat needed to survive. Game laws were enacted to confine hunting to specified regular seasons. Deer were brought in from other parts of the country by game managers to replenish the herds. Today, white-tailed deer are the most commonly seen large mammal on the Parkway.

Inside the stone visitor center, open May to October, are a Parkway information desk and displays accompanied by an interpretive area addressing riverine topics of natural and cultural history. The large grassy area below the visitor center and beside the James River makes a great picnic spot, and picnic tables and grills abound. Two trails—the Trail of Trees and the James River Canal Trail—lead from the visitor center.

## Trail of Trees

The half-mile, self-guided Trail of Trees offers access to the trees that grow in the vicinity. Signs identify trees and shrubs along the path. You shouldn't miss the commanding view of the James River, even if you don't hike the half-mile lower loop. Follow the side of the loop closest to the river, and in 0.1 mile, reach a stone overlook with the noteworthy vista.

## James River Canal

The 0.2-mile James River Canal Trail leads across the footbridge under the Parkway bridge. As high above the water as this footbridge is, it was washed out by a flood in 1985, and another flood in 1992 nearly reached it. On the other side of the bridge, the trail leads to a lock remaining from the James River and Kanawha Canal. This lock was built between 1845 and 1851.

The idea of a canal connecting the James River with the New River (then known as the Great Kanawha River) and ultimately the Ohio River was championed by George Washington in the 1780s. At that time navigable waterways were the only means to connect distant regions. By November of 1851, the 206.5-mile section from Richmond to Buchanan was completed. That was as far as the canal would ever get. The canal was often damaged during spring rains and never proved to be profitable.

At the time it was completed, 90 locks with a total of 728 feet of lift existed between Richmond and Buchanan. Passage on the Richmond-to-Lynchburg section cost $7.50 per person one way, but children and servants were billed half price. The trip took 33 hours going upstream and 31.5 hours downstream.

On January 21, 1854, the *Clinton* sank in the James near this lock. Frank Padget, a slave who saw the wreck from the shore, jumped into the frigid water and pulled several crew members to shore. As he went back for the last member of the crew in sight, both men drowned. A monument built later to honor Padget is located upriver from the lock.

The canal was an important lifeline for Confederate troops during the Civil War and was severely damaged by the Union army. It stayed in use until 1880, when it was bought by the Richmond and Allegheny Railroad (predecessor of the Chesapeake & Ohio). They built railroad lines, which are still in use, along the canal towpath.

## 63.9
### US 501
Drive 2 miles east to Big Island and another 20 miles to Lynchburg. It is 9 miles west to Glasgow.

## 69.1
### James River Valley Parking Area
This overlook offers nice winter views of the James River Valley, as well as a picnic table.

## 71.0
### Petite's Gap—USFS 35
Parking for the Appalachian Trail is 50 yards west; Cave Mountain Lake Recreation Area, 8 miles. This was originally Poteet's Gap, named after the owner of the land here, but by 1850 it was already showing up on maps as Petite's Gap.

In this area you will notice extensive tree damage, the result of southern pine beetles.

## 72.6
### View Terrapin Mountain
Terrapin Mountain is one of the many landmarks in the area that was named for its resemblance to an animal or object; in this case, the mountain bears a striking resemblance to its namesake.

## 74.7
### Thunder Ridge Overlook
Thunder Ridge Trail, a 0.1-mile loop, leads to an overlook with views of the Arnold Valley and the towns of

Glasgow and Natural Bridge and provides access to the Appalachian Trail. Walk 0.25 miles south to the Hunting Creek Trail, a scenic 2-mile (one way) trail, which switchbacks gently down the mountain through tunnels of rhododendrons.

## 75.2
### View Arnold Valley
The valley was named for Steve Arnold, who settled here about 1749. Views include Devil's Hopper and Snake Den Ridge. A second pulloff is 0.1 mile south.

## 76.5
### Apple Orchard Overlook
An exhibit here provides information on Apple Orchard Mountain. Wind, ice, and snow have pruned the lichen-covered northern red oak on the mountain, giving it the appearance of an old apple orchard. Seen from the Parkway, the large, golf ball–shaped tower you see on the summit is radar used by the FAA for air-traffic control. From the 1950s to the 1970s, the U.S. Air Force stationed 120 people here.

## 76.7
### Highest Point on the Blue Ridge Parkway in Virginia
The elevation is 3,950 feet at Apple Orchard Mountain.

## 78.4
### Sunset Field Overlook—USFS 812
Here, enjoy wonderful views of Virginia's Great Valley.

The Apple Orchard Falls Trail (strenuous) is here. The 1.2-mile trail heads downhill (2,000 feet!) to the 150-foot falls. You can also access the Appalachian Trail here. The road, also called Parker's Gap Road, leads to North Creek Campground straight ahead. The right fork is an FAA access road that is gated before it reaches the summit.

The Appalachian Trail is a couple hundred yards down Parker's Gap Road (or take Apple Orchard Falls Trail 0.25 miles to its junction with the A.T.). Heading north on the Appalachian Trail, it is a moderate day hike over Apple Orchard Mountain. This hike features great views from the summit and an interesting rock formation called The Guillotine, through which the trail passes before meeting the Parkway about 2 miles from the trailhead (milepost 76.3). Walk 0.25 miles south along the Parkway to reach the Apple Orchard Overlook.

This is also a great area for wildflowers, with mayapples

A number of birds use the sky above the Blue Ridge Parkway as an aerial highway, following the ridges of the Appalachians north in the spring and south in the fall.

In spring, hawks migrate inconspicuously (unlike other birds), and in fall, they soar along the Blue Ridge in flocks. The hawks travel with the weather, benefiting from both the northerly winds and the sun. When the sun heats the cliffs and rock outcrops along the Blue Ridge and its parallel ranges, the rocks warm the air above them. This air, in turn, rises in forceful drafts called thermals. The hawks rise with the drafts, soaring and spiraling on motionless wings. By the time the air currents cool and no longer provide lift for the hawks, the birds are thousands of feet in the air and can drift southward to the next updraft. Using this method of transportation,

blooming in late March, bloodroots and trilliums in April, azaleas and wild geraniums in May, and rhododendrons and mountain laurels from late May through June.

### 79.7
### Onion Mountain Overlook
The 0.2-mile Onion Mountain Loop Trail leads through interesting formations of lichen-covered boulders as well as a maze of rhododendrons and mountain laurels, which are particularly impressive in June. The mountain was named for its extensive beds of wild onions, also known as ramps, leeks, and ingins.

### 79.9
### View Black Rock Hill
Black Rock is visible as a large rock formation just right of center but is often obscured by summer plant growth. It is composed of diorite, a feldspar-rich, quartz-poor rock that gets its dark color from the mineral hornblende.

### 81.9
### View Headforemost Mountain
An exhibit about the tulip poplar tree is located here. The mountain can be seen, often through a frame of leaves, ahead. The other side of the mountain falls suddenly, or headforemost, to the valley below, hence its name.

### 83.1
### Falling Water Cascades Parking Area
Falling Water–Flat Top National Recreation Trail begins here. Falling Water Cascades Trail loops 1.6 miles north to this waterfall. A connector trail at this area leads 0.8 miles to the Flat Top trailhead and parking area.

hawks can travel hundreds of miles each day.

A number of good hawk-watching spots are along the Blue Ridge Parkway from mid- to late September. In Virginia, Rockfish Gap (milepost 0.0), Buena Vista Overlook (milepost 45.7), Harvey's Knob Overlook (milepost 95.3), and The Saddle (milepost 168.0) are all excellent hawk-watching locations. In North Carolina, you can spy hawks at Mahogany Rock Overlook (milepost 235.0), Craggy Pinnacle (milepost 364.1), Mills Valley Overlook (milepost 404.5), and Devil's Courthouse (milepost 422.4). The most common hawk you will see is the broad-winged, but the sharp-shinned and the red-tailed are also frequently seen, and you may catch a glimpse of a peregrine falcon or even a bald eagle.

## 83.5

### Flat Top Trail

Flat Top Trail leads 4.4 miles across Flat Top Mountain (elevation 4,001 feet) to the Peaks of Otter picnic area. The mountain was once called Round Top because it appears more round than flat from some views.

## 85.6

### Peaks of Otter Lodge

Open year-round, the 62-room lodge features a restaurant with a lounge, a coffee shop, and a gift shop. Behind the lodge is Abbott Lake, named for Stanley William Abbott, the Parkway's first resident landscape architect and planner. The 24-acre lake features a one-mile loop and is stocked with smallmouth bass, catfish, golden shiners, sunfish, and blue gill. When the lake was constructed, archaeological artifacts dating back more than 8,000 years were discovered on the site. For additional information, call (800) 542-5927 or (540) 586-1081 or visit www.peaksofotter.com.

> *"Sharp Top once marked the northern boundary of the Cherokee Nation"*

## 85.9

### Peaks of Otter Visitor Center, Campground, and VA 43

A number of theories claim to explain how Peaks of Otter came by its unusual name. One theory suggests that the name came from the Cherokee word *ottari*, which means "high places." It is also possible that the name originates from the Otter River, whose headwaters are found in the Peaks area on the eastern side of the mountains. A third guess is that the mountain was named for the Otter Highlands by Scottish settlers who felt that Sharp Top resembled the mountains of their homeland. The Peaks are made up of three mountains: Sharp Top (3,875 feet), Flat Top (4,001 feet), and Harkening Hill (3,375 feet). The Peaks of Otter Visitor Center is located at 2,545 feet.

Information signs are posted in the area on Sharp Top Mountain, Big Springs, Polly Wood's Ordinary, Weather at Work (the boulders of Sharp Top), Sharp Top Summit, Johnson Farm, and Elk Run Trail.

The visitor center offers restrooms, water, and an amphitheater. The museum, refurbished in 2003, features exhibits on the natural and cultural features that have made this area a recreational destination since the 1880s. Open May through October, the visitor center sells postcards, books, and other items reflecting nature and local-interest themes. Bus rides to within 1,500 feet of the Sharp Top summit are available at a station not far from the visitor center. This area includes a gas station, 62-table picnic area, camp store, and a 141-site campground that features 53 RV sites.

The Peaks of Otter area is also the habitat of the Peaks of Otter salamander that can be found only within a 10-mile radius of the Peaks. There are 34 kinds of salamanders living in the southern Appalachians, more than in any other region in the world.

VA 43 leads east to Bedford.

## Trails

A number of trails are in the Peaks of Otter area.

**Sharp Top Trail**    The trail begins at the camp store (across the Parkway from the visitor center) and leads 1.6 miles to the summit of Sharp Top. This strenuous hike with a 1,400-foot elevation gain offers a panoramic view from the summit. In season, a bus offers both one-way and round-trip transportation to the top. Long predating the Parkway, Sharp Top Trail has guided visitors to the mountain summit since the 19th century. Each year, thousands still make the pilgrimage and are rewarded with views of the Piedmont and the town of Bedford to the east; Harkening Hill, Harvey's Knob, the James River Valley, and the Alleghenies to the west; and the Blue Ridge Parkway as it winds its way along the backbone of the Blue Ridge Mountains to the north and south. More specifically, view Wheat's Valley, Flat Top Mountain, and Thunder Ridge to the north, and Buzzard's Roost to the south. Abbott Lake is behind Peaks of Otter Lodge nearly 1,600 feet below.

**Elk Run Loop Trail**  This is a short, 0.8-mile loop that begins behind the visitor center and features a self-guided tour on the forest community.

**Harkening Hill Loop Trail**  Running 3.3 miles, this trail begins behind the visitor center and takes you over sometimes steep and strenuous terrain to the top of the ridge with views of Johnson Farm. This area was farmed until the 1940s, and the fields are still kept open by the park service. You will also pass by old fruit trees before reaching the 900-foot side trail to Balance Rock, a large boulder balanced on a smaller rock.

**Johnson Farm Trail**  This trail to Johnson Farm intersects Harkening Hill Loop Trail twice. Johnson Farm Loop Trail can be accessed from the visitor center by a 1-mile trail. The restored farm looks as it did in the 1930s and has living-history demonstrations in the summer.

Johnson Farmhouse in the
Peaks of Otter Area
(MP 85.9)

### Johnson Farm

The Peaks of Otter community was established in 1766 when Thomas Wood moved to the area from Pennsylvania. He settled in a cabin on what is now the Johnson Farm, passing the farming tradition from generation to generation until 1852, when the Johnson family bought the original four-room cabin from James Joplin.

John T. and Mary Elizabeth Johnson had 13 children, who helped them plow, plant, and harvest the land. Tomatoes, potatoes, and cabbage were their cash crops, and they grew a number of other vegetables for their own use. John's son Jason bought the farm from his father and brought the house to its present appearance, adding a dining room, kitchen, porches, and storage rooms. Jason and Jenny Johnson raised nine children. The last Johnsons to live in the house were Jason's daughter Callie and her husband, Mack Bryant. The Bryants also raised nine children and lived at Johnson Farm through the 1930s.

Today, Johnson Farm has been restored to look much as it did in the 1930s, with the barn, house, other buildings, and garden open for exhibit. Living-history demonstrations in the summer include planting and harvesting the garden, making a patchwork quilt, and more. Don't be surprised if you are asked to lend a hand.

### Peaks of Otter/Mons Community

The Johnsons were very much connected to the community of Mons and the Peaks area, which centered on approximately 20 families living within a 2-mile radius. The community supported a large hotel, an elementary school, and combination church/Oddfellows Hall. The church and hall were once located on the site of the current lodge's restaurant.

The success of the Johnsons and other farming families was dependent on the tourist trade at the local hotel. The Johnsons and the Bryants often took overflow guests from Hotel Mons, and they and other families also provided the hotel with food and labor. Known as Otter Peaks Hotel from the time it was built in 1857 until it burned down in 1870, the hotel was run by Benjamin Wilkes and his son Leyburn. The hotel was rebuilt after the fire, accommodating 40 guests and staff. It was closed in 1936 and dismantled in the early 1940s.

### Sharp Top/Harkening Hill/Flat Top

The Peaks of Otter is made up of three mountains— Sharp Top, Harkening Hill, and Flat Top.

Sharp Top Peak was one of the reasons so many tourists

were attracted to the Peaks of Otter area. A hike to its summit was a pleasant way to spend a summer's day. Five buildings were built atop the peak, including a luncheon counter to provide food for hungry hikers and structures for housing hikers, particularly during inclement weather. Supplies were carried up the mountain by horse or mule, and water was collected in rain barrels atop the summit.

Once hikers had made the strenuous climb to the summit, they were charged at the gatehouse before being permitted entrance to the summit compound. Adults were charged 50 cents, children 25 cents. For a number of years, a large rock (20- to 30-feet high) was a major attraction atop the summit. This balanced rock was a constant amusement for the hiking public who were interested only in unbalancing it. They finally succeeded, dislodging the boulder around 1820. It tumbled off the peak and imbedded itself in a spur of the mountain. In 1852, the boulder was blasted into fragments and one of the larger pieces sent off to Washington, D.C., to be used in the construction of the Washington Monument. It can be seen today at the 12th stairway landing in the west wall. The rock bears this inscription:

"From Otter's summit,
Virginia's loftiest peak,
To crown a monument
To Virginia's noblest son."

Sharp Top is also historically significant in that it once marked the northern boundary of the Cherokee Nation.

Harkening Hill, the third of the three peaks, also has a source of debate regarding its name. One possibility suggests that *harkening* is a corruption of *hurricane*. On the other hand, it might have actually come from the word *harkening*, either from farmers who climbed the hill to harken to the sound of their cows' bells or from hunters who climbed the hill to harken to the sound of their hounds. A third possibility is that it is a mispronunciation of Harkeny, perhaps one of the first owners of the mountain.

Flat Top was once called Round Top because it appears more round than flat from some views. Flat Top Trail leads 4.4 miles from the Peaks of Otter picnic area over Flat Top Mountain (elevation 4,001 feet).

### Polly Wood's Ordinary

The Peaks community also features Polly Wood's Ordinary, an inn that furnished simple lodging and meals for travelers from 1834 until 1860. The building was originally located just above the dam of Abbott Lake but has since been moved 200 yards to its current position. Living-history demonstrations are occasionally held here during the summer.

The inn was started by Mary "Polly" Wood upon the death of her husband in 1830. Left only a portion of 90 acres (the land owned by her husband was divided among Polly and their nine children), she could not keep going financially by farming only. After several years, she finally opened her home, a small log cabin with a single door and window in front, as the simplest of inns, known as an "ordinary" at the time. It served travelers on the Buchanan to Liberty Turnpike. Her daughter Mary and Mary's husband, Nicholas Wilkerson, helped her run the inn. Polly died circa 1855 (records are unclear), and her daughter ran the inn another five years before closing its simple door.

### 89.1
### Powell's Gap
This relatively low gap (elevation 1,916 feet) was once the site of a buffalo path that was later used by Native Americans and then white settlers as a shortcut across the mountains from the eastern trading path to the Great Valley's warrior path.

### 89.4
### View Upper Goose Creek
The valley below, called Goose Creek Valley, was once a large marsh frequented by migrating duck and geese.

### 90.0
### View Porter Mountain
The oak-chestnut forest, sometimes known as a mixed hardwood forest, is the most common along the Blue Ridge Parkway. An excellent example of such type of forest can be found at this overlook where white, northern red, black, scarlet, and chestnut oaks can all be found. Although this forest is called an oak-chestnut forest, you will no longer find the American chestnut here.

### 91.0
### Bearwallow Gap—VA 695
Here, the Appalachian Trail passes beneath the Parkway, paralleling it for the next 7 miles south. VA 695 leads 10 miles east to Montvale. Buchanan and access to I-81 is 5 miles west on VA 43.

## 91.8

**Mills Gap Parking Area**

A picnic table is available at this pulloff. The A.T. parallels and crosses the Parkway here.

## 92.1

**Purgatory Mountain Parking Area**

Enjoy a view of Purgatory Mountain, which rises more than 3,000 feet. The mountain was named after a creek located in the town below.

## 92.5

**Sharp Top Parking Area**

This overlook offers a view of Sharp Top Mountain, one of the three prominent summits of the Peaks of Otter. (Sharp Top, right; Harkening Hill, center; and Flat Top, left.) There is a wayside panel here on the Appalachian Trail, which passes through the parking area.

## 93.1

**Bobblet's Gap Overlook**

The Bobblet family cemetery sits on a knoll, which the overlook encircles. It is the family cemetery of Will Bobblet, who farmed the land here for a number of years in the early 1900s before heading to the valley town of Buchanan on the western side of the mountains. He left behind seven members of his family in the tiny graveyard. Picnic tables and views of Sharp Top Mountain can be found here.

## 95.2

**Pine Tree Overlook**

A number of tall pitch pines were the reason for the name, but lightning has since caused their demise. You can still enjoy a wonderful view of Goose Creek Valley.

## 95.3

**Harvey's Knob Overlook**

In September, thousands of hawks migrate down the Blue Ridge, catching warm updrafts from the valleys and heading toward their wintering grounds in South America. People often gather with binoculars and lawn chairs to watch birds of prey flying along the mountain chain. You might even catch a glimpse of a bald eagle. Access to the A.T.

## 95.9

**Montvale Overlook**

This parking area overlooks the Montvale community. Spec

Mine Trail is 200 feet south of this overlook. Keep an eye out for a sign marking the trailhead on the right bank. You will also find a picnic table and access to the A.T. here.

## 96.2
### Iron Mine Hollow Parking Area
Low-grade iron ore was mined in this general area during the Civil War and through the early 1900s. You might even locate some old mine entrances within the first half mile of the Spec Mine Trail. To access the trail, park at the Montvale Overlook (milepost 95.9) and walk south about 200 feet. Watch for a sign marking the trailhead on the right bank.

## 96.4
### Iron Mine Hollow Parking Area
This area is known for its pre–Civil War mining.

## 97.0
### View Taylor Mountain
The big mountain straight off the overlook is Porter's Mountain; Taylor Mountain is to the left. Hikers may access the A.T. here.

## 97.7
### Black Horse Gap
This gap (elevation 2,402 feet) was once a stagecoach route across the mountains.

## 99.6
### The Great Valley Overlook
A nearby sign interprets the view of the Great Valley. The Alleghenies border the valley to the west; the Blue Ridge Mountains are to the east.

## 100.9
### The Quarry Overlook
Below, view an active quarry operated by the Blue Ridge Stone Corporation. Dolomite, the rock mined here, is used for surfacing roads.

# Roanoke
# and the Vicinity

• • • • • • • • • • • • • • • • • • • • • • • •

This section travels through the largest urban area along the Parkway—the city of Roanoke, often called the Capitol of the Blue Ridge. Because of nearby urban development and the lack of public land, this section of the Parkway has a different feel—the presence of a city. Roanoke, which is often surprisingly close to the motor road, dominates many of the scenes from Parkway overlooks along this section. (Find the best view of the city from the top of Mill Mountain.)

In the 1740s, Mark Evans and Tasker Tosh came from Pennsylvania and settled in the center of the Great Valley, near a large salty marsh. Many animals came to lick the salt from the marsh, lending Roanoke its first name of Big Lick. When the railroad came in 1852 and bypassed the valley's first village, everyone moved to the tracks. In 1882, the town became Roanoke and grew rapidly around a railroad hub that serviced Shenandoah Valley Railroad, which later became Norfolk & Western.

Roanoke was the name given to the river and the county. The name was derived from the native word *Rawrenock*, which was a string of shells that Native Americans wore around their neck and used in trading with the white settlers. Today, the city of Roanoke remains an industrial city with a strong tie to the railroad, now Norfolk Southern.

Roanoke marks a change in topography along the Parkway. Steep and narrow mountains give way to broad rolling hills as the motor road heads south over the Roanoke River. To the north of town, spurs run off a predominant ridge (known as Brushy Mountain) and curve to parallel the Parkway, often exceeding it in height. Views to the east reveal the Piedmont, and views to the west reveal the Great Valley and beyond it, the Alleghenies. South of the city, this main ridge transforms into an elongated plateau with isolated knobs called monadnocks.

As the Parkway swings around the east side of Roanoke, you will find the road relatively flat and straight. Four exits off the Parkway take you into the city: US 460 (milepost 105.8), VA 24 (milepost 112.2), Mill Mountain Spur Road (milepost 120.4), and US 220 (milepost 121.4).

Don't miss the following highlights in downtown Roanoke: Science Museum of Western Virginia, Roanoke Museum of Fine Arts, Virginia Museum of Transportation, Mill Mountain Theater, and Roanoke Valley History Museum. Be sure to visit downtown Roanoke's historic open-air market, where farmers in the area have sold their crops for more than 120 years.

Pine Mountain Overlook on a spur road (MP 115.0)

This stretch of the Parkway provides a recreational outlet for people living in Roanoke. Recreation includes fishing along the Roanoke River, hang gliding from Roanoke Mountain, hiking on the Appalachian Trail, and utilizing this section's unique Roanoke Valley Horse Trail.

Two spur roads lead off the Parkway—Virginia's Explore Park Visitor Center (milepost 115.0) and Mill Mountain Park (milepost 120.4). At Mill Mountain Park, you can visit a zoo and the Discovery Center and have a look at the famous Roanoke Star. And while Virginia's Explore Park has been closed for the foreseeable future, the Blue Ridge Parkway Visitor Center located there remains open.

### 105.8
### US 460
Nine miles west to Roanoke; 21 miles east to Bedford.

### 106.9
### N & W Railroad Overlook
When steam locomotives come into Roanoke for various events, people often gather at this overlook, which offers a beautiful view of the railroad grade. During the age of the iron horse, Norfolk & Western, now Norfolk Southern, carried bituminous coal from the mines in West Virginia to the ports of Hampton Roads, Virginia. The region's coal played a significant role in the exploitation and industrialization of Appalachia, and today Norfolk Southern plays a significant role in the city's economy.

The importance of this railroad is celebrated annually at the Railway Festival (Columbus Day weekend). The festival includes a model railroad fair. At the Virginia Museum of Transportation, which interprets the history of the railroad, you will find railroad artifacts and photos, plus vintage electric locomotives and classic diesels. The museum is located downtown in a restored railway freight station next to the Norfolk Southern mainline.

### 107.1
### View Coyner Mountain
Winter views to the west from this parking area.

### 109.8
### Read Mountain Overlook
The mountain is named for David Read, who farmed in the area in the mid-1800s.

During the past century, disease and pest problems have changed the forests of the Blue Ridge dramatically. From the chestnut blight to gypsy moths, each hazard has taken out different species of trees.

In the 1890s, the Blue Ridge Mountains were dominated by oak-chestnut forests, with about 40 percent of the trees being American chestnut. At the turn of the 20th century, a fungus called chestnut blight was discovered at the Bronx Zoo. The blight quickly spread from imported chestnuts to the native American variety. By 1930, trees as far south as western North Carolina had been decimated. While the root systems have managed to survive, the shoots rarely reach maturity, as the trees are attacked by the blight before they achieve significant growth. A few chestnut trees have been able to survive the blight and reproduce. Researchers are working with these trees and the blight-resistant strain that is approximately 90 percent American chestnut. Hopefully, science can help bring the chestnut trees back to their former glory.

As you drive along the Parkway, particularly in the area of milepost 71.0, you may notice that the landscape is scarred by an unusual number of dead pine trees. In the early 1990s,

### 110.6

#### Stewarts Knob Overlook

Stewarts Knob Trail (0.1 mile) leads to a bench where you can relax and enjoy a view of downtown Roanoke. Stewarts Knob is the first peak south of Roanoke Valley. This overlook is the northernmost trailhead for Roanoke Valley Horse Trail, which parallels the Parkway from milepost 110.6 to 121.4, although you must return to the Parkway to cross the Roanoke River at milepost 114.7.

### 112.2

#### VA 24

Five miles to Roanoke; 2 miles to Vinton; 4 miles to Stewartsville.

### 112.9

#### Roanoke Basin Overlook

Roanoke Valley Birding Club builds and maintains bluebird houses along this stretch of the Parkway to help the native bluebird compete with starlings and house sparrows.

### 114.7

#### Roanoke River Bridge

The Roanoke River flows into Smith Mountain Lake. The river offers good trout fishing upstream from this point, these trees in the Glenwood Ranger District of George Washington and Jefferson national forests were attacked by southern pine beetles. About the size of a grain of rice, the southern pine beetle prefers loblolly and shortleaf pine hosts, but all southern pines may be attacked. The trees are destroyed when thousands of these mating beetles quickly infest individual trees. The beetles excavate S-shaped egg galleries in which eggs are deposited in niches on either side of the gallery. Once these galleries are opened, death results either from girdling of the main stem, or from the effects of the blue-stain fungus introduced by the beetle.

Once these tunnels are opened, the blue-stain fungus invades the tree and kills it. The life cycle of southern pine beetles is only one month, and the trees can be attacked by five to six generations of the insect in a single growing season. The U.S. Forest Service is now using logging, hand spraying, and cutting and burning to bring the pest under control.

Other recent problems are gypsy moths, which are eating the forest's leaf canopy; dogwood anthracnose, which is killing dogwood trees in forested areas; and hemlock woolly adelgid, which is causing the death of eastern and Carolina hemlocks.

and good bass (striped and white) fishing below here to the lake, especially in the spring and fall. The elevation at the river is 825 feet.

## 114.9

### Roanoke River Parking Area

Roanoke River Trail (0.4-mile loop, easy) is a self-guided trail that takes you into the gorge and to a patio overlook on the banks of the Roanoke River.

## 115.0

### Virginia's Explore Park

A 1.5-mile spur road connects the Blue Ridge Parkway to the former Virginia's Explore Park, which has been closed due to lack of funding. The three overlooks along this road offer views of the Black Creek Valley and the foothills of eastern Roanoke.

While the park has been closed, plans are underway to create another attraction at the end of this spur road—Blue Ridge America. The proposed park will include hundreds of luxury hotel rooms, cabins, and even tree houses that will be designed to blend in with the mountain and river scenery.

The attraction will also feature restaurants, live theater, excursions to Smith Mountain Lake, an equestrian center, retail shops, a golf course, conference center, and spa. According to the plan, an overhead gondola system will be built to transport visitors through the park and to a zip line, said to be the world's longest. For more information on the park's progress, see www.blueridgeamerica.com.

## Blue Ridge Parkway Visitor Center

Through the cooperative partnership of the Blue Ridge Parkway, Roanoke County, and Virginia's Explore Park, this building provides educational and interpretive exhibits on the Roanoke region and the Blue Ridge Parkway.

### 120.3

## Roanoke Mountain Loop

Seven overlooks are located on this 4-mile loop road. The overlooks near the summit of Roanoke Mountain offer views of Roanoke Valley, the city of Roanoke, and Mill Mountain. Roanoke Mountain Summit Trail (0.1 mile) goes to the summit of Roanoke Mountain. Depending on the wind, hang gliders gather near the top of Roanoke Mountain. (Hang gliding is allowed by permit only.)

### 120.4
## Mill Mountain Spur Road

#### 1.1
## Chestnut Ridge Overlook

Here, find a map of Chestnut Ridge Trail (5.4-mile loop, moderate). The trail, which is a particularly rewarding section of Roanoke Valley Horse Trail, loops around the campground, and side trails to the campground allow for hikes of various lengths.

#### 1.3
## Roanoke Mountain Campground

This campground is conveniently located on the way to Roanoke. Several sites of old iron mines are located near the campground. Local musicians perform traditional and bluegrass music Sunday evenings from June through October.

#### 2.5
## Mill Mountain Zoo

Take a left to visit the Mill Mountain Zoo, Mill Mountain Discovery Center, Regional Information Center, and the Roanoke Star. Continue ahead to follow J.B. Fishburn Parkway down Mill Mountain to the city of Roanoke (2 miles).

The Blue Ridge Zoological Society of Virginia, Inc., operates Mill Mountain Zoo, a 10-acre site with 46 species of native and exotic animals, including hawks, Siberian tigers, and red pandas. A contact area houses small mammals, and an amphitheater hosts interpretive programs in the summer. The zoo is open year-round, and an entrance fee is charged. For more information, see www.mmzoo.org. The Discovery Center was created to offer an awareness and appreciation of Mill Mountain using environmental education exhibits, programs, and classes. Since its inception, more than 140 educational programs, day camps, and community events have been offered at the facility. Programs focus on wildlife, geology, ecology, mountain flora, fauna, natural history, and human impact.

In 1949, the Roanoke Star was erected on top of Mill Mountain to represent Roanoke's zest for progress. Consequently, Roanoke is often referred to as the Star City of the South. The Roanoke Star is the world's largest man-made star: tower height, 100 feet; star height, 88.5 feet; weight, 10,000 pounds. The illuminated star can be seen 60 miles away.

> **"**
> the Roanoke Star
> is the world's largest
> manufactured star
> **"**

## 121.4
### US 220
Five miles west to Roanoke; 21 miles east to Rocky Mount. This milepost is the southernmost trailhead for Roanoke Valley Horse Trail.

## 123.2
### Buck Mountain Overlook
Buck Mountain Trail (0.5-mile loop, moderate) leads to a bench on the top of the mountain, which offers views of the mountains surrounding southern Roanoke Valley.

## 126.6
### Mason's Knob Overlook
John Mason lived near the knob at the time of the French and Indian War in the mid-1700s.

## 128.7
### Metz Run Overlook
This overlook was named for the cascade on Metz Run, which is located in a small valley across the road and 100 feet south.

### 129.3
### Poages Mill Overlook

Elijah Poage operated a gristmill and sawmill here in the mid- to late 1800s. He was a cabinetmaker, undertaker, and justice of the peace, as well as a mill owner.

### 129.6
### Roanoke Valley Overlook

Here, find one of the best views of the development in Roanoke Valley. Come at night to see the lights. A sign details the railroad heritage of Roanoke and the city's historic market.

### 129.9
### Lost Mountain Overlook

The mountain is still there, but the origin of its name has been lost to time.

### 133.6
### View Bull Run Knob

The ridgeline at this overlook resembles a bull.

### 134.9
### Poor Mountain Overlook

This mountain is not named for a man of small means, but for an officer, Major Poore, who served in the French and Indian War.

# Settlers on the Landscape: Agriculture and Rural Life

• • • • • • • • • • • • • • • • • • • •

Many stories of mountain life along the Blue Ridge tell of an illiterate people living way up in the mountains, scraping by on subsistence farming. Though such farmers could be found in these mountains, this is an inaccurate stereotype, one inconsistent with the lives of most people of the Blue Ridge Mountains. Along this section of the Parkway, progressive buildings stand testament to lives far different than the stereotype. The Parkway reveals a region whose history cannot be told by a few rough-hewn log cabins alone. The industry, education, and surprisingly diverse daily lives of the people along the Parkway are seen at Mabry Mill, Kelley Schoolhouse, Orlena Puckett's cabin, Flat Top Manor, and other interpretive sites on this section of the Parkway.

Mabry Mill was built in 1910 by Edwin B. Mabry. He saved his earnings in the coal fields to build a gristmill, sawmill, and wheelwright shop. The mill became a focal point of the Meadows of Dan community. The Mabry Mill area (milepost 176.2) is now one of the most heavily visited sites on the Parkway and has interpretive displays on rural life in Appalachia. The dam at Rakes Mill Pond (milepost 162.4) is another remnant not just of industry but also of advertising ingenuity, as an interpretive sign at the dam explains.

The Kelley Schoolhouse located just off the Parkway (milepost 149.1) is the only school building remaining along the Parkway's route. When Floyd County, Virginia, where the school is located, incorporated in 1831, the justices of the County Court set out that first year to establish a system of free schools. In 1877, the Locust Grove trustees bought the land for $15 from the Kelley family and built a one-room schoolhouse.

Patterns of daily life changed rapidly in the late 19th century when outside interests began to look to the Blue Ridge Mountain's natural resources to supply materials for the burgeoning growth of towns along the eastern seaboard. The timber and (to the west of the Blue Ridge) coal barons built railroad tracks into the mountains and began buying land. Initially, many tenant farmers were delighted to work for wages, and settlers were happy to sell some of their acreage for cash, which they used for buying the goods they couldn't make, grow, or barter. Often they would sell some ridgetop or steep sloping acreage that couldn't be farmed anyway, but eventually this practice had a detrimental effect. Over time, many families traded too much land for cash. Strapped for resources, families were forced to seek employment to earn the things they could no longer supply for themselves. In other areas of the mountains, farmers would sell their mineral rights and keep the ownership of the property. The way the mineral rights deeds were written, the surface could not be used for farming or residential use. Once the railroad came in and the owners of the mineral rights staked their claims, all the farmers owned was the tax burden.

Much of the timbered land of the Blue Ridge was bought by the U.S. Forest Service and National Park Service to create Shenandoah and Great Smoky Mountains national parks, the Blue Ridge Parkway, Pisgah National Forest in North Carolina, and George Washington National Forest in Virginia. By that time, in the 1930s, daily life along the Blue Ridge was forever changed from an agriculture-based economy to one based on a mix of agriculture, industry, and tourism.

Off the Parkway in Floyd and Galax, Virginia, and Sparta, North Carolina, you'll find an intact slice of rural Appalachia. These small towns and surrounding farms make for a nice side trip in the area. The nationally renowned Old Fiddler's Convention is held annually in Galax, which is west of the Parkway from milepost 215.8.

The North Carolina towns of Boone and Blowing Rock have a lot to offer area visitors, including many shops, museums, parks, and an outdoor drama. A regional tourist information center is located west of the Parkway on US 321/221 (milepost 291.8) between Boone and Blowing Rock.

## 135.7
### Cemetery
The family cemetery of the Rev. Daniel H. Shaver (1860-1949) and his wives, Coredellia Wimmer (1861-1912) and Patra Mills (1878-1970), is located on the west side of the Parkway. Children and other family members are buried here as well.

## 135.9
### US 221—Adney Gap
Nineteen miles to Roanoke. The gap was named for Thomas Adney, who ran a hemp mill in this gap in the late 1700s.

## 138.5
### Sweet Annie Hollow
Who was Annie and why did people think she was so sweet? The story handed down since the American Revolution tells of a widow who had a home in this hollow, where soldiers were frequent guests. Her neighbors took a dim view of the impropriety and ran her off, but Sweet Annie, as the soldiers knew her, has lived on in the name of her hollow.

## 139.0
### View Cahas Mountain
For the next 215 miles south, the Parkway closely follows the eastern continental divide, with almost all of the creeks on the east side of the Parkway flowing eventually into the Atlantic, and nearly all those on the west leading to the Gulf of Mexico. To the north, the divide crests to the west, in the Allegheny Mountains, and waters flow across the Blue Ridge en route to the Atlantic.

## 142.5
### Cemetery
The family cemetery of Jonas (1887–1952) and Mellawalka (1887–1950) Wilson is on the west side of the Parkway. Their infant children are also buried here.

**143.9**
**View Devils Backbone**
View western Piedmont of Virginia and Devils Backbone.

**144.8**
**Pine Spur Overlook**
A picnic table and view of western Piedmont are here.

**149.1**
**Kelley Schoolhouse**

While not currently open to the public, the nearby Kelley Schoolhouse offers an interesting look into life before the Parkway. The school was originally housed in a one-room building constructed in 1877. It did not have running water or electricity, and the school did not get an outhouse until 1917. Children walked as far as 2 miles to get to the school, which was open even in the worst weather. A typical school year ran from October through May, but often saw low attendance during good weather, as students stayed at home to help their family run the farm. Class started at 9 a.m. and ended at 4 p.m. The school offered reading and writing to young children, while older children studied English, arithmetic, geography, and the history of Virginia and the United States. Teachers typically served for one or two years before moving on. Because no substitutes were available, teachers taught even when sick.

The original one-room schoolhouse couldn't meet the needs of the growing student enrollment, and the existing two-room schoolhouse was built on the lot in 1923. The school was still in operation when the Parkway was built, and most of the school's land was sold to make way for the road. As roads in the area improved, the school system was consolidated, and Kelley Schoolhouse closed in 1939.

The former school building became Pate's Grocery Store in 1939, after Virgie Pate bought the schoolhouse at auction. The Pates made a number of additions and improvements to the building, adding electricity and an upstairs living area. In the 1950s, the Pates bought a television for the store, and neighbors often gathered in the evening to watch it. The Pates sold the store in 1972. Mr. O. B. Ware ran the store, now called Ye Old Country Store, until he sold the building to the Parkway in 1984.

**150.9**
**VA 681/VA 640**
Floyd-Franklin Turnpike (VA 681) is to the west, and Five Mile Mountain Road (VA 640) is to the east.

## 154.1 ![symbol1] ![symbol2]
### Smart View Overlook

Though there is a pretty, or smart, view from this parking area, the overlook takes its name from the Smart, Virginia, post office that once served this area.

## 154.5
### Smart View Parking Area

A road leads from the parking lot on the Parkway to the Smart View picnic area. On the right, between the Parkway and the picnic area, is a small parking lot at Trail Cabin on the right. The Trail family lived in this log building in the 1890s. Sometime after 1925, the door and floor were removed, and the cabin was used as a barn. At the time the Trail family built their hand-hewn cabin, American chestnut trees towered over the area. The trees provided wood for buildings and fences, dye for clothes, and food for people and hogs. Farmers also sold nuts for up to 28 cents a pound. The chestnut blight of the 20th century decimated the great trees.

Smart View Loop Trail can be accessed from this parking lot, as well as from the picnic area. The 2.6-mile trail encircles the Smart View area. The picnic area offers tables and restroom facilities. A picnic shelter and a fireplace are also available on a first-come, first-serve basis.

Shaver Cemetery
(MP 135.7)

Both rambling stone walls and miles of split-rail fences can be seen along the Parkway. At milepost 8.8, you can observe a good example of the remnants of "hog walls," which were built in the early 1800s by slaves of valley plantations. The stone walls were mended only once a year (in winter) and were used to control the wanderings of feral hogs that foraged in the forests for acorns and chestnuts.

Most of the split-rail fences you will see along the Parkway were constructed of chestnut. The mountaineers used many styles of construction, including snake, post and rail, buck, and picket. An example of these types of fences can be found at Groundhog Mountain (milepost 188.8).

### 155.3
### VA 793/VA 680
Four miles east on VA 793 to Endicott; VA 680 travels west.

### 157.6
### Shortts Knob Overlook
Named for Amos B. Shortt, a local trapper who sold and traded pelts in this area. He was known for carrying a bag, a cane, and a .22 revolver when he was checking his traps. If the animal wasn't already dead, he would use the cane to kill it. He only used the gun when absolutely necessary, out of fear of ruining the animal's pelt.

### 162.4
### Rakes Mill Pond Overlook
An interpretive sign at this overlook tells the story of this mill and its owner, Jarmon Rakes. He built the dam in the early 1800s and is remembered for his unique arrangement of allowing only customers to fish for brook trout in his pond. There was no extra charge to try your luck at fishing while waiting for your grist.

### 165.3
### Tuggle Gap—VA 8
The road leads 6 miles west to Floyd and another 22 miles to I-81. Go east 21 miles to reach Stuart and another 7 miles to Fairy Stone State Park. The gap is named for a minister by the name of Tuggle who lived near the gap at the time of the American Revolution.

### 165.6
### Cemetery
Access to the large local cemetery on the east side of the Parkway is from Tuggle Gap.

## 167.1 ![icon][icon]

### Rocky Knob

Rocky Knob has a campground with tent and trailer sites, restrooms, and a dump station for RVs. The campfire circle accommodates up to 150 campers.

### Rock Castle Gorge Trail

This 10.8-mile trail drops 1,800 feet from the Parkway into the gorge with many steep sections of trail and passes through an area rich in biological diversity. A former district ranger reports 28 species of fern and 45 species of trees that are native to the trail.

## 168.0 ![icon]

### The Saddle

This outstanding view is a popular destination for hawk spotters in the fall. Rock Castle Gorge Trail passes by this parking area. From here it is 0.3 miles to an old Appalachian Trail shelter on Rock Castle Trail. An interpretive sign describes the view from this overlook.

## 168.8 ![icon]

### Rock Castle Gorge Overlook

You can access the 10.8-mile Rock Castle Gorge Trail from this parking lot.

Dam at Rakes Mill Pond Overlook (MP 162.4)

### 169.0

## Rocky Knob Visitor Center and Picnic Area

An information station and an interpretive sales area are located at the turnoff for the picnic area. You'll find a good selection of traditional Appalachian music and items related to gristmills and other mountain industries. The picnic area has 72 tables, restrooms, a phone, and a picnic shelter. Two trails can be accessed from the picnic area, the 3.1-mile Black Ridge Trail and the 1-mile Rocky Knob Picnic Area Loop Trail.

### 169.1

## Twelve O'Clock Knob Overlook

Access to Rock Castle Gorge Trail from this parking area.

### 174.1

## VA 758/Woodberry Road

Highway 758 leads east to the Rocky Knob Housekeeping Cabins 1 mile away. For reservations and information, call (540) 593-3503. Built in the 1930s by the Civilian Conservation Corps, the cabins are open from May 1 through November 1.

### 175.9

## VA 603 (gravel road)

The Mabry Mill overflow parking area is located here.

### 176.2

## Mabry Mill

A much-admired landmark, Mabry Mill is known as the most photographed spot on the Parkway. Crowds converge on the idyllic setting on summer weekends to admire the handiwork and get a glimpse at the lifestyle of Ed and Lizzie Mabry.

> **" Mabry Mill is the most photographed spot on the Parkway "**

After saving his hard-earned money from the coal fields of West Virginia, Ed Mabry moved here and, circa 1910, built the now-famous gristmill, sawmill, and wheelwright shop to serve the Meadows of Dan community. With his wife, Lizzie, Ed ran the mill until his death in 1936. He is remembered in the community as a man who could repair anything you could break.

For the first 15 or more years of the mill's operation, work was steady and life was good for the Mabrys. They built a two-story frame house near the mill. This house was later removed by National Park Service planners and, in the 1950s, the present log cabin was moved here.

Ed injured his back in the mid-1920s, and infrequent

rains made running the mill unpredictable in the 1930s. He died in 1936, with the mill in poor condition. As fate would have it, that was the same year the Parkway right-of-way was being acquired in Virginia. Lore suggests Parkway architect Stanley Abbott fell in love with the picturesque mill and not only acquired the property but also slated the mill for preservation instead of removal.

A restaurant with a gift shop, restrooms, and phone is a short distance from the well-known landmark.

A half-mile-long walkway leads from the main parking area to the mill and then beyond to several interesting exhibits of rural life. In the summer and fall, the mill is in operation, and demonstrations are often given in the blacksmith shop. In the fall, apple butter–making demonstrations are along the trail and weaving demonstrations are held in the cabin.

On Sunday afternoons there is often an informal music gathering in the open area near the blacksmith shop. Area musicians play traditional mountain music for locals and tourists alike.

### 176.3
#### Mabry Mill Overflow Parking
Park here when the Mabry Mill main parking area is full.

A weaving demonstration
at Mabry Mill (MP 176.2)

Log cabins, such as the Ramsey Cabin (milepost 5.8), Trail Cabin (milepost 154.5), and Brinegar Cabin (milepost 238.5), were still common along the Blue Ridge Mountains in the late 1800s. Trees felled on the site would be squared off with a broad ax and adze, which left their traces in the rough-hewn walls of the cabin. After they were cut and hewn, the logs were dovetailed together at the notches in the end to form the walls of the cabin. The roofs were typically made of cedar shakes hand split on the site. The spaces between the logs were chinked with rock and mud. In the early days, cabins were built with shutters instead of glazed windows. The ever-present fireplace served both to cook meals and heat the home in winter.

## 177.7
### Meadows of Dan—US 58

This intersection with US 58 leads east 16 miles to Stuart, Virginia, and 21 miles west to Hillsville, Virginia. The Meadows of Dan, a farm community, derives its name from the Old Testament, as does nearby Dan Creek and the Pinnacles of Dan.

## 179.3
### Round Meadow Overlook

The Round Meadow Creek Loop Trail offers a moderate half-mile hike.

## 179.4
### Round Meadow Viaduct

The Parkway passes over Round Meadow Creek, which is 110 feet below the viaduct.

## 180.1
### VA 600

Mayberry Presbyterian Church and Cemetery (east) is one of two churches along the Parkway that were built by the Rev. Bob Childress. His churches feature a signature rock facade. Childress, born in 1890, averaged 50,000 miles a year as he traveled the Blue Ridge to minister to his 14 churches. His death in 1956 was mourned by all his parishioners, and his life was later memorialized in a book by Michael E. Davids, *The Man Who Moved a Mountain.*

## 183.4
### Pinnacles of Dan Gap

When the route of the Appalachian Trail was being selected through this area in the late 1920s, the Pinnacles of Dan were included as a joke. The chairman of the

As a family prospered, they would often add a second cabin alongside and connect the two with a common roof. The breezeway formed between the two cabins is where these dogtrot cabins derived their name. Clapboard siding became increasingly popular in the late 1800s and early 1900s. By the time the Parkway was built in the 1930s, cabins had been replaced by frame houses as the dominant home style. Parkway planners, however, preserved many cabins and demolished or moved some of the newer houses to preserve the pioneer look they wanted for the new roadway.

Appalachian Trail Conference, Myron Avery, was renowned for his trail building in Maine and northern Virginia. To see how he would react, local hikers told Avery the route of the A.T. was to go over the jagged Pinnacles of Dan. Avery thought that looked like a fine idea and blazed a trail up and over the rocky peaks. The trail moved to the west when the Parkway came through.

## 188.8

### Groundhog Mountain

The picnic area features tables, a comfort station, and a short trail from the parking area to an observation tower. The tower boasts an excellent 360-degree view, and there is a cemetery on an island in the parking area, with the graves of Emerline, Emmer, and Billy Mart Bowman. Burial dates range from 1916 to 1981. An exhibit on rail fences explains how the rails were used to bound pastures. Made largely of chestnut, the fences along the Parkway are of three basic designs—snake, post and rail, and buck. This picnic area features an exhibit of the three aforementioned rail fences, as well as picket fences.

## 189.1

### View Pilot Mountain

The quartzite sides of Pilot Mountain can be seen 25 miles to the south across the North Carolina piedmont.

## 189.9

### Puckett Cabin Parking Area

A wayside exhibit provides information on the history of Orlena Puckett. The cabin here was actually home to Orlena's sister-in-law Betty, who lived here with her children after her husband died from wounds received in the Civil War. Orlena's cabin was located adjacent to

The mountains that make up the backbone of the Blue Ridge Parkway are all part of the central and southern Appalachians, which extend from southern Pennsylvania to northern Georgia. In Virginia, the Parkway sticks to the narrow northern Blue Ridge all the way to the Roanoke area. South of the Roanoke River, the ridge widens into a broad and rolling plateau. From the gently rolling farmland of southern Virginia, the Parkway climbs into mountains in excess of 6,000 feet in elevation. As the Parkway rolls toward North Carolina, the landscape becomes more rugged, and after it enters the state, it is dominated by ranges with other names besides Blue Ridge—the Blacks, Craggies, Pisgah Ledge, and Plott Balsams. These mountain ranges in North Carolina are among the more than half dozen that crisscross the Blue Ridge like the rungs of a ladder.

The Parkway leaves the Blue Ridge at milepost 354.0, heading west into the cross ranges. The Parkway reaches the Black Mountains first, passing very near Mount Mitchell (6,684 feet), the highest peak east of the Mississippi. From the Blacks, the Parkway passes through the Craggies, Pisgah Ledge, and the Plott Balsams, reaching its highest point at Richland Balsam (6,047 feet).

Betty's. Orlena Puckett delivered more than 1,000 babies during her career as a midwife. Using only soap, water, and a nip of whiskey flavored with camphor, Orlena was said to have never lost a child or mother due to any fault of her own.

One tale recounts that when the weather was so "rough and slick" that "a body couldn't keep to his feet," Orlena pounded nails through the soles of her shoes to make her way to an expectant mother. She began her practice around 1890; she charged $6 per birth "when times was good" and $1 when they weren't. She also bartered her services when paying cash was a problem. Orlena delivered her last infant in 1939 at the age of 102. Of the 24 children Orlena herself bore, not one made it past infancy; the oldest survived just past two years of age.

### 191.9
### Private Road

Bluemont Presbyterian Church and Cemetery are to the east. Bluemont is another of the Rev. Bob Childress's churches (see milepost 180.1).

### 193.0
### Volunteer Gap

This gap provides a particularly good example of the

agricultural use of the land, as well as a view of the overall characteristic landscape.

## 196.9
### Cemetery
The cemetery on the west side of the Parkway bears three marked graves and a number indicated only by stones. The three marked graves are those of W. H. and Hester Hayes (1895, 1908) and Bulah Edwards (1929).

## 199.5
### Fancy Gap—US 52
Mt. Airy is 14 miles east; Hillsville is 9 miles west. Lodging, gas stations, and restaurants are available at this exit.

## 202.8
### Granite Quarry Overlook
An exhibit here explains Mount Airy granite and includes a sample of the granite. Take in the views here of the North Carolina Piedmont, including Hanging Rock State Park and Pilot Mountain State Park.

## 203.9
### View Piedmont
Another excellent view of the North Carolina Piedmont, 1,900 feet below.

## 213.3
### VA 612–Blue Ridge Music Center
This joint venture between the National Park Service and the National Council for the Traditional Arts features a visitor center, trails, and most important, the Blue Ridge Music Center Amphitheater.

The amphitheater offers concerts May through October, and except for the occasional big-name bands, concerts are free and feature regional old-time and bluegrass musicians.

The visitor center is open 9 a.m. to 5 p.m. daily, May through October, and during most evening concerts. The visitor center hosts a mix of temporary and permanent exhibits, which trace the diversity of American roots music to this area. A permanent exhibit at this site is in the works. It will trace the history of this music through local artists back to the creation of the music created generations ago by persons from Europe and West Africa, and it will show how this type of music has been kept in America.

High Meadow Trail is 1.35 miles one-way. The easy

Born near what is now the city of Reading, Pennsylvania, on November 2, 1734, Daniel Boone was the 6th of 11 children in a Quaker farming family. He had no regular schooling but was taught by an aunt how to read and write. Boone grew up with firsthand experience with cattle, horses, wagons, blacksmithing, weaving, hunting, and trapping. He received a new rifle for his 12th birthday, and from then on spent long days in the woods, learning to shoot, trap, and develop his strength and agility.

When he was 16, his family sold their farm and moved to the Yadkin Valley of North Carolina. There, they staked out another farm and settled down. It was in the mountains of Appalachia that Boone honed his famous hunting skills, trading animal skins for lead, gunpowder, salt, and other items. Although Boone loved the beauty of the mountains,

**"**

*construction of the Blue Ridge Parkway began at Cumberland Knob in 1935*

**"**

trail takes you through a hayfield and a wetland with an abundance of wildflowers and birds. It also winds through a forest with a rich display of rhododendrons, ferns, and rock outcrops. Two junctions for Fisher Peak Loop join this trail. You may turn onto the loop trail, follow High Meadow Trail to visit the music center's visitor center, or return to the trailhead from these points.

Fisher Peak Loop Trail is a moderate 2.24-mile trail beginning at one of its junctions with High Meadow Trail. The trail winds up the side of Fisher Peak through a variety of vegetation. At the lower elevation, the trail follows a stream through mixed pine and hardwoods. Higher up, the blooms of azaleas, mountain laurels, and Catawba rhododendrons provide a spectacular display in May. They give way to diverse second-growth forests of oak, poplar, maple, and sourwood trees. Look for abundant signs of animal life—woodpecker holes, deer tracks, and turkey dust baths.

For more information, call (276) 236-5309 or (540) 745-9662 or visit www.blueridgemusiccenter.org.

**215.9**
**VA 89**
Mt. Airy, NC, is 22 miles to the east; Galax, VA, 7 miles to the west.

his interests lay elsewhere—the wilderness west of Virginia. Five years after moving to the Yadkin Valley, Boone left to take part in the French and Indian War. He later returned to the valley to marry his childhood sweetheart, Rebecca Bryan.

In 1767, he journeyed through the rugged Appalachians and reached the Kentucky wilderness. Boone later helped cut the Wilderness Road west 300 miles from eastern Virginia through the Cumberland Gap to the Kentucky River. The settlement at the end of the road was named Boonesboro in his honor. He moved his family to Kentucky and later to the Louisiana Territory before ending up in Missouri with his grandchildren, where he died on September 26, 1820, at the age of 85. Boone's Trace, at milepost 285.1, is where the frontiersman is said to have crossed the Blue Ridge.

## 216.9
## Virginia-North Carolina State Line

## 217.5
## Cumberland Knob Picnic Area and Visitor Center

In addition to the Cumberland Knob Visitor Center, this area also features a 33-site picnic area, interpretive sales area, comfort stations, hiking trails and a trail shelter, and cemetery. It is said that the area received its name from William Augustus, Duke of Cumberland. The son of King George III, the duke defeated Bonnie Prince Charlie at the Battle of Culloden in Scotland in April 1746. Virginia explorer Dr. Thomas Walker gave the area its name in the 1750s while on an exploratory trip for his patron, the duke of Cumberland.

Cumberland Knob is where Blue Ridge Parkway construction began in 1935. More than 60 years ago, the first bit of the 469-mile Parkway was cut at the Virginia-North Carolina line, with more than 100 men involved in the construction. The first section built ran 12.49 miles south from the state line.

Behind the visitor center, you will find arrows etched into the flagstone patio pointing to mountain peaks visible from the viewpoint.

### Trails

Cumberland Knob has two hiking trails: a 0.5-mile leg stretcher and a strenuous 2-mile hike. Cumberland

Knob Trail begins on the paved trail near the visitor center, looping through the picnic area to the Cumberland Knob Overlook Shelter. Gully Creek Trail starts at the visitor center or at Cumberland Knob Loop Trail. It is a strenuous hike with several climbs and an 800-foot elevation change.

## 218.6

### Fox Hunters Paradise Parking Overlook

At the exhibit located here, learn about Fox Hunters Paradise, the knoll low on the ridge where hunters once sat listening by the fire as they followed the chase in the lowlands. The short Fox Hunters Paradise Trail (0.2 miles) leads to an outstanding view that extends to Winston-Salem, North Carolina, on clear days. Fisher's Peak is just ahead and to the left; Pilot Mountain is in the far distance.

## 223.1

### Big Pine Creek

Big Pine Creek parallels the Parkway for several miles and is a popular trout-fishing spot.

## 225.3

### Hare Mill Pond

The owners of the grist- and sawmills that once stood on this pond bought rabbits, or hares, from trappers to sell at a regional market, giving the mill and pond their name.

## 229.7

### US 21

Drive west 7 miles to reach Sparta, North Carolina, or east 25 miles to Elkin, North Carolina. Little Glade Creek is a popular trout-fishing spot. In 1998, it was restored after receiving major damage from soil erosion that harmed water quality and fish habitat.

## 230.1

### Little Glade Mill Pond

Here, find five picnic tables and an easy, 0.3-mile hike around the pond. Trout fishing is popular in the creek behind the pond. The pond itself is a good place for children to catch bream and to view snapping turtles, newts, frogs, and dragonflies.

## 232.5

### Stone Mountain

There is a wayside exhibit here on Stone Mountain (elevation 3,879 feet), a true monadnock. The oval-shaped mass of light-gray granite, 500 to 600 feet in elevation, can be viewed from here. The mountain is part of the 13,378-acre Stone Mountain State Park, where activities include climbing, hiking, camping, and fishing. Picnic table here.

### 233.7
### Bullhead Mountain Overlook
Bullhead Mountain is 3,784 feet in elevation.

### 235.0
### Mahogany Rock Overlook
This is an excellent hawk-watching spot in September and October—broad-winged, sharp-shinned, and red-tailed hawks all fly over this pass. A picnic table is here.

### 235.7
### Devils Garden Overlook
This rough and rocky area is so called because only the Devil could admire it as a garden. Rattlesnakes and copperheads are often found in this area.

Observation tower at Groundhog Mountain (MP 188.8)

Groundhogs, the mammals you are very likely to see on the Parkway, call warning with a shrill whistle, earning it the name *whistle pig*. Groundhogs are members of the squirrel family, and although most are brown, their coloring ranges from red to gray or almost black. One-third of the adult groundhog's two-foot-long body is tail. Keep an eye on the shoulder of the Parkway, where groundhogs often feed on roadside vegetation.

Groundhogs are common along the Parkway because the roadway provides them with both food and shelter. The grass and other plants along the roadside furnish groundhogs with their favorite food, while the holes and spaces between the large rocks under the roadbed are ideal for a den. Groundhogs dig two dens: a winter den with good drainage and a spring and summer den near food. They aren't big travelers, always

### 237.1
### Air Bellows Gap

This gap was the site of an early road across the Blue Ridge Mountains. The gap is near the former community of Air Bellows.

### 238.5
### Brinegar Cabin Parking Overlook

When his family moved here from North Wilkesboro, North Carolina, Martin Brinegar built this two-room log cabin as well as a springhouse, root cellar, and barn. The Brinegars had three children (a fourth died in infancy), who helped raise hogs, cows, and chickens. The family also had an orchard, cornfield, vegetable garden, flax field, and a bee gum for honey. Martin's wife, Caroline, used a four-poster loom she brought with her from North Carolina to weave linen and wool cloth for the family's clothes.

To earn money, Martin sold shoes he made by hand for about $1 a pair. To supplement this income, the family also sold mayapple and blackberry roots, as well as soap. The Brinegars were active churchgoers, and Caroline was left a widow in 1925 after Martin went to church in a terrible rainstorm. He caught pneumonia and died. Caroline stayed 10 more years, and then sold the property to make way for the Blue Ridge Parkway, taking her loom with her. The origin of the current four-poster loom is unknown.

Long after the property was sold, the Brinegar family continued to meet here for family reunions. The remaining close to the entrance of their burrow.

The groundhog is one of the park's true hibernators. Prodded by their biological clocks, groundhogs head for their burrows in October and hibernate until late February. Their respiration rate and body temperature drop, and their heart only beats about five times per minute. Because their only source of energy comes from stored fat, groundhogs lose a quarter of their body weight over the winter.

About every 10 days, groundhogs wake and stretch, taking in deep breaths to clear their respiratory system. On mild winter days in the South, you might even see a groundhog emerging from its burrow. If it happens to be aboveground in February, the groundhog's reactions may help some folks make predictions about the weather, a practice that has earned this mammal a place on our calendars—Groundhog Day.

reunions eventually grew into an annual festival held the first weekend in April. Traditional crafts, including spinning, weaving, and open-hearth cooking, are featured.

In addition to the cabin, the area also has an exhibit on Appalachian gardens, which illustrates some of the vegetables grown by the Brinegars. You'll also find exhibits about making linsey-woolsey and the building of the cabin, as well as about the springhouse and root cellar.

## Trails

Two trails—the 4.3-mile Cedar Ridge Trail and the 7.5-mile Bluff Mountain Trail—begin at Brinegar Cabin. Cedar Ridge Trail skirts the northern side of the Doughton Park boundary to Grassy Gap Fire Road. (Grassy Gap Fire Road heads west 6.5 miles back to the Parkway.) There is a 2,000-foot elevation change on this hike. Bluff Mountain Trail, though longer, covers more level terrain and parallels the Parkway.

## Enter Doughton Park

When you view the peaks and hollows at Doughton Park, you will catch your breath at the tenacity of the mountaineers who once settled here. Basin Cove, home to the Caudill family, still features their century-old cabin, which was one of the few structures to survive a devastating flood in 1916. Nestled between Fodderstack and Bluff Ridge, the Caudills' home was part of a thriving mountain community at Basin Cove. The banks of Basin Cove Creek were home to more than 75 families, including members of the Caudill family, as well as the Blevins, Pikes, Tilleys, and Wagoners. The flood chased away most of the families.

James Harrison Caudill, a 16-year-old from Elkin, North Carolina, was the first to settle in the area, arriving after the Civil War had ended. Caudill sired 22 children, 11 boys and 11 girls, by his first two wives. His third wife, Zephyr Pike, outlived him, even though Caudill lived to the age of 98.

The remaining cabin, which can be seen from Wildcat Rocks, belonged to Caudill's son Martin, who raised 16 children. The community of Basin Cove is an excellent example of the many small communities that thrived along the Blue Ridge. The community ran both a school and a church—Basin Creek School and Basin Creek Union Baptist Church. Basin Creek alone produced four lawyers and a number of preachers and teachers. The community also boasted a post office and general store.

Unfortunately, the flood of 1916 washed away all but the original Caudill home, Martin's home, and the church. Twelve members of the community were drowned in the flood, fields were washed down to bare rock, and the survivors were forced to abandon the cove. Even the Caudills left the cove a month after the flood. When the land was purchased by Robert Doughton in 1930, he had the church torn down for its lumber.

The park was named for Doughton, a member of the U.S. House of Representatives. He served as chairman of the Ways and Means Committee from 1933 to 1947 and from 1949 to 1953, and was instrumental in the development of the Blue Ridge Parkway.

Although originally called Bluff Park, the park was renamed later for "Farmer Bob" Doughton, the "Father of the Blue Ridge Parkway." Well known and well loved in his hometown of Sparta, North Carolina, Doughton was famous for everything from his size 15 shoes to eating apples with every meal to his many accomplishments in Congress. Although he did not arrive in Washington until he was 47, he spent the next 43 years there, until he died at the age of 90.

If you hike along the trails in the park (particularly Basin Creek Trail and Grassy Gap Fire Road), you will find the remains of the once-flourishing community of Basin Cove—an empty cabin, old foundations, deteriorating fences, and lonely chimneys. The eastern edge of Doughton Park borders on the Thurmon Chatham game lands and Stone Mountain State Park. With its more than 20,000 acres of undeveloped forest land, this area offers

*" originally called Bluff Park, Doughton Park was renamed after "Farmer Bob" Doughton, a congressman instrumental in getting the Parkway built "*

you chances to spot any number of animals, including deer, squirrels, foxes, rabbits, raccoon, bears, or even bob-cats. Wildcats were once a real threat to the domesticated animals of the cove, particularly the sheep, and were the source of such names as Wildcat Rocks and Sheeps Hell.

## 239.2
## Doughton Park Campground
Tent sites and restrooms, as well as a campfire circle, can be found at this campground. The RV campground on the other side of the Parkway (east) has trailer sites and a comfort station.

## 240.7
## Parking Area (West)
Access Bluff Mountain Trail here.

## 241.1
## Doughton Park Concession Area
To the west, you will find Bluffs Coffee Shop and a service station, and to the east, a picnic area and the 24-room Bluffs Lodge and Restaurant (call (336) 372-4499), along with a gift and craft shop.

Also to the east is Wildcat Rocks Overlook. It, like the lodge, is on the left fork of the road. A short trail leads up to the overlook, where a sign describes the homestead of Martin Caudill, which can be seen in the valley below the overlook.

### Trails
Fodder Stack Trail, a 1-mile moderate hike, begins here. The trail leads to Fodder Stack Mountain. Taking the right fork in the road brings you to the picnic area, where you can hike up the grassy slope to a small shelter located on Bluff Ridge Primitive Trail. There is a good view from the shelter.

*"during the winter, ice accumulation can be as thick as one inch along portions of the Parkway"*

## 242.0
## Ice Rock
This large section of rock was exposed when the road was cut. Runoff from this rock sometimes freezes in winter as it crosses the road. Ice accumulations can be as thick as one inch across the Parkway.

## 242.4
## Alligator Back
This overlook offers an exhibit on raptors and mammals of the area. Once called varmints and killed on sight, hawks, owls, bears, foxes, and snakes are now recognized

as an important part of our environment. You can also access Bluff Mountain Trail here, which is 100 feet down the stone steps.

### 243.4
**Bluffs View Overlook**
Access Bluff Mountain Trail here.

### 243.7
**Grassy Gap**
Here is the terminus of Grassy Gap Fire Road (6.5 miles), as well as access to Bluff Mountain Trail. From Grassy Gap Fire Road, you can also reach Basin Creek Trail, which follows the cascading waterfalls of Basin Creek 3.3 miles to the Caudill Cabin. More than 100 years old, the former home of the Martin Caudill family was once part of a thriving community and was one of the few to withstand the flood of 1916.

### 244.5
**Cemetery (east)**
The oldest marked grave in this family plot (which includes Blevins, Wyatt, Moxley, and Brooks family members) is of William P. Blevins (1850–1883).

### 244.7
**Basin Cove Overlook**
Hikers can access Bluff Mountain Trail and Flat Rock Ridge Trail here. The latter begins in the mountaintop meadow and ends 5 miles later at Basin Cove Creek near Grassy Gap Fire Road. The elevation here is 3,312 feet. A sign here tells about the Doughton Park trail system.

### 252.3
**Sheets Cabin**
This cabin was built by Jess Sheets circa 1815. Many generations of the Sheets family lived here until 1940.

### 252.8
**Sheets Gap Overlook**
Parking area with picnic tables.

### 258.7
**Northwest Trading Post—NC 1632**
This gift shop specializes in handmade crafts from more than 500 active artists from 11 counties in northwest North Carolina. Available are wood carvings, handmade toys, knitting, hand crochet, books, antiques, folk toys, baskets, brooms, canes, weaving, pine-needle crafts,

pottery, musical instruments, metal crafts, and more. The Trading Post also offers homemade foods, including hams, pickles and relishes, dried foods, biscuits, and other baked goods. A Parkway visitor center, picnic tables, and restrooms are available here as well. For more information, call (336) 982-2543.

## 260.3
### Jumpinoff Rock Parking Area
Here, find two picnic tables and easy access to Jumpinoff Rock Trail, a half-mile easy hike that leads to an overlook on sheer rock cliffs above a forested valley. The elevation here is 3,312 feet.

## 261.2
### Horse Gap—NC 16
North Wilkesboro is 20 miles to the east; West Jefferson is 13 miles west. There is access to the Mountains-to-Sea Trail here.

## 264.4
### The Lump Overlook
This overlook has an exhibit on Tom Dula, the inspiration for the song "Hang Down Your Head, Tom Dooley." Dula was hanged in neighboring Wilkes County in 1868 for the murder of one of his lovers. Tradition says that he composed the song while in prison. The song suggests that another jealous lover was responsible for the murder, although Dula neglected to give history her name.

Lump Trail (0.3 miles) features views of the vast panorama of the foothills below and the Grandfather Mountain area. The elevation here is 3,465 feet. A picnic table is available here.

## 266.8
### View Mount Jefferson
An exhibit here tells about Mount Jefferson (4,683 feet), formerly known as Negro Mountain. A cave near the top of the mountain is said to have been used by slaves fleeing to Ohio before the Civil War. The mountain is now part of the 474-acre Mount Jefferson State Park. The mountain was renamed for the town of Jefferson in Ashe County when the park was created.

## 267.8
### Betseys Rock Falls
Look to your left for a view of the falls.

Many landowners were happy to sell rights-of-way for the Parkway when land was being purchased by Virginia and North Carolina in the 1930s. Of course, many didn't want to sell or held out for sentimental reasons. In his book *The Blue Ridge Parkway,* Dr. Harley Jolley recounts the story of one such woman who didn't mind moving if she wouldn't have to break family tradition. She had spent every night of her life in the house since her husband had carried her across the

### 269.8
### Phillips Gap
This gap is named for Caleb Phillips, who raised 24 children here.

### 271.9
### Cascades Parking Overlook—E. B. Jeffress Park Area
The Cascades area has picnic tables, a comfort station, and a water fountain. A 0.6-mile trail leads to an overlook of the Cascades and a trail to Cool Springs Baptist Church (0.5 miles) and the Jesse Brown Cabin.

An exhibit provides information on E. B. Jeffress Park, which was named in honor of the chairman of the North Carolina State Highway and Public Works Commission in 1933. A supporter of the Blue Ridge Parkway project, Jeffress led the fight to keep the Parkway from becoming a toll road.

### 272.4
### Cool Springs Baptist Church/Jesse Brown Cabin
A church exhibit explains how the small shelter was used only in times of inclement weather. Mountain families gathered here to listen to Bill Church and Willie Lee preach. The two men would then spend the night at the nearby Brown cabin.

The cabin itself was built by Brown prior to 1840. Originally located about 0.5 miles up the hollow from its present position, the cabin was later moved to Tompkins Knob Overlook, then once again (to its present position) by Aaron Church in 1905 to bring it closer to its water source. Two generations of the Church family lived in the cabin from the 1890s. It was also once known as the Old Walker Place.

The church also started out at Tompkins Knob Overlook (it was moved by the National Park Service). The Church family may have used the structure as a barn. It has been restored twice, and its original appearance is now disputed.

threshold as a young bride. To keep tradition intact, the state of Virginia used a resourceful solution and sawed the house in half. While one half of the house was being moved to the new site, the tradition-conscious homeowner slept in the other half. The next day she moved into half of her old home in its new location, while state workers brought the other half to join her.

## 272.5
### Tompkins Knob Overlook
Here is another trail to the Jesse Brown Cabin and Cool Springs Baptist Church (only 200 yards away). A 0.6-mile trail leads to Tompkins Knob.

## 274.3
### Elk Mountain
Elk Mountain (3,795 feet) was named for the elk that once roamed the southern Appalachians.

## 276.4
### Deep Gap—US 421
A part of a Civil War trench remains in the triangle formed by the Parkway here. Federal Major General George Stoneman had earthworks built in this gap to protect his lines of communication during the spring of 1865. Elevation here is 3,142 feet.

## 277.3
### View Stony Fork Valley
View the valley, 900 feet below. The elevation is 3,405 feet.

## 277.9
### View Osborne Mountain
Winter views.

## 278.3
### Carroll Gap Overlook
The elevation is 3,430 feet.

## 281.4
### Grandview Overlook
See a "grand view" of the community of Triplett. Elevation here is 3,240 feet.

## 285.1
### Boone's Trace
Local tradition places this area on the route Daniel Boone traveled to Kentucky. A historical marker and bronze plaque honor Boone. A picnic table is here.

### 285.5
### Bamboo Gap
The gap was named for the nearby community of Bamboo. Elevation is 3,262 feet.

### 288.0
### Aho Gap
The gap was named for the nearby Aho community. Lore says that a group of men gathered to select a name for their community but were unable to agree upon a name. It was then decided that the next word spoken by any one of them would be accepted. After a long silence, B. B. Dougherty arose, stretched, and said, "Aho!"

### 289.5
### Raven Rock Overlook
Raven Rock Overlook is one of the grandest places to watch the sun set. It looks westward as the sun sets behind Grandmother, Sugar, and Beech mountains. The elevation here is 3,810 feet; Raven Rock is 3,913 feet.

### 289.8
### Yadkin Valley Overlook
The Yadkin Valley was the home of Daniel Boone. The Yadkin River was first called the Saponi by John Lawson in 1709, but by 1733 it was known both as the Saponi and the Yadkin. While the Saponi tribe lived in the area, the meaning of Yadkin is uncertain. The elevation here is 3,830 feet.

### 290.4
### Thunder Hill Overlook
This overlook is one of the region's most active overlooks. It is ideal for ham radio reception as well as sailplaning, and is a stupendous place to watch the sun rise.

### 291.8
### US 321 and US 221
Boone, North Carolina, lies 8 miles west; go east 2 miles to Blowing Rock, North Carolina. The regional information center in Boone provides travel information.

**"**
*Daniel Boone moved with his family to the Yadkin Valley in 1750*
**"**

# Grandfather and the Black Mountains

• • • • • • • • • • • • • • • • • • • •

Because of the donations made by John D. Rockefeller, Jr., and the philanthropic heirs of Moses H. Cone and Julian Price, this section boasts three unique recreation areas. At the Moses H. Cone Estate, you will find a stately mansion housing a craft center, grounds with remnants of old apple orchards, man-made lakes, and miles of carriage roads that provide plenty of recreation. In Price Park, you will find a picnic area and campground situated near the 47-acre Price Lake, which offers fishing and canoe rentals. Down the Linville Falls spur road, you will find the most spectacular waterfall on the Blue Ridge Parkway. Linville Falls plunges into a 1,500-foot-deep gorge. The area offers a variety of hiking trails, as well as a campground along the Linville River. All of these recreation areas are the result of the kindness of wealthy families who believed in the importance of nature and its preservation.

At the beginning of this section, you will find Flat Top Manor. Moses H. Cone, whose mammoth textile mills produced high-quality denim, purchased 3,500 acres near Blowing Rock during the 1890s and early 1900s. He built a summer mansion for his family. Cone died in 1908, only a few years after completing Flat Top Manor. His wife, Bertha, lived another 39 years. By mutual agreement, she and Moses's brothers and sisters left the estate to Moses H. Cone Memorial Hospital of Greensboro, North Carolina. In 1949, not long after her death, the hospital donated the estate to the park service to be used for public recreation in memory of Mr. Cone. Be sure to visit the family cemetery on the hike to Flat Top Tower. There, you'll find the newspaper obituary inscribed on the back of his tombstone.

Julian Price, founder of Jefferson Standard Life, one of the nation's major insurance companies, purchased land in the late 1930s to use as a retreat for his employees. Price was killed in an automobile crash in 1946, and the company donated the tract to the park service in July 1949 for use as a recreation area. Boone Fork was dammed to form Price Lake, a memorial to a man who deeply loved this land.

In 1951, John D. Rockefeller, Jr., donated $95,000 to the National Park Service and the U.S. Forest Service to acquire land in Linville Gorge. Linville Falls Recreation Area was created when an additional 535 acres, the cascade tract, was added to the Parkway in April 1952.

In addition to the three recreation areas, this stretch offers two of the high country's most famous highlights— the Linn Cove Viaduct and Grandfather Mountain. The

**Equestrians in front of Moses H. Cone Memorial Park (MP 294.0)**

Linn Cove Viaduct, an engineering masterpiece, is a road built away from the mountain in partial suspension to protect the fragile ecosystem along Grandfather's girth. A thrill to drive across and a wonder to hike beneath, the viaduct was part of the "missing link" that held up completion of the Blue Ridge Parkway until 1987.

Rising to an elevation of 5,964 feet, Grandfather Mountain watches over the Parkway for most of this section. The motor road hugs Grandfather's slopes for about 6 miles, from Cold Prong Pond Overlook (milepost 299.0) to Beacon Heights (milepost 305.2). Enjoy a grand view from Grandfather Mountain Parking Overlook (milepost 306.6), and visit the private park at the top of the mountain by leaving the Parkway on US 221 (milepost 305.1).

This section contains the Parkway's newest long trail, officially completed in 1993. Tanawha Trail stretches 13.5 miles from Boone Fork Overlook (milepost 297.2) to Beacon Heights parking area (milepost 305.2), and many overlooks north of Linn Cove provide access points to the trail. The construction of Tanawha Trail, like the viaduct, was complicated by the fragile ecosystem along the flanks of Grandfather Mountain. To protect the delicate environment, the unique construction includes arched bridges and boardwalks extending up to 200 feet; for a natural effect, the building materials used blend with the landscape.

*Tanawha*, a Cherokee word used to describe Grandfather Mountain, means "fabulous hawk or eagle"; a feather represents the Tanawha on trail signs. Tanawha hugs the southeastern slope of Grandfather Mountain for most of its length and offers boulder fields and rhododendron thickets, hardwood and evergreen forests, and clear mountain streams. For more information, pick up a National Park Service trail map detailing Tanawha Trail.

The area around Gillespie Gap is rich in geologic diversity created millions of years ago when molten rock flowed through the area. The many veins of igneous rock, formed when the molten rock cooled, later were metamorphosed by the extreme heat and pressure under the earth's crust. These veins are where miners and rock hounds alike now find quartz, garnet, mica, rubies, and emeralds. You can look at excellent examples of many of the gems and minerals for which the area is known at the Museum of North Carolina Minerals just off the Parkway at milepost 330.9.

Along this section of the Parkway, you will get a good view of the tallest mountains in the Appalachians—the

**"**
*the Blue Ridge Parkway was finally completed in 1987 with the construction of the Linn Cove Viaduct*
**"**

In 1942, a sandwich shop and picnic supply store opened at Cumberland Knob (milepost 217.5) to serve Parkway visitors. Sandwiches, canned goods, and gasoline were sold from the front flip-up window of a lean-to shed. The business was run by the fledgling National Park Concessions, Inc., contracted by the park service to provide essential facilities and accommodations for those traveling the Parkway.

The second concession (and the first lodging facility) to open on the Parkway—Bluffs Lodge and Coffee Shop—was built by the park service in 1949 at Doughton Park (milepost 241.1) and was also operated by National Park Concessions, Inc. The 1950s brought the modest addition of Rough-it Camp, which later became Rocky Knob Housekeeping Cabins (milepost 174.1), and a gas station at Crabtree Meadows (milepost 297.0).

Black Mountains. The major peaks of the Black Mountains are all above 6,000 feet. At milepost 342.2, an interpretive sign points out all of the peaks in the range.

In this section the Blue Ridge Parkway leaves the mountains for which it was named and passes through several other ranges before reaching the Smokies. At Ridge Junction Overlook, also called Black Mountain Gap (milepost 355.3), the Parkway skirts the Black Mountains. The Black Mountains feature some of the highest peaks east of the Mississippi River, including the highest, Mount Mitchell, which towers 6,684 feet above sea level. The Parkway leaves the eastern rampart of the Blacks for the Great Craggies with its huge heath-covered balds. From the Craggies, the Parkway descends to the French Broad River Valley, home to the city of Asheville.

### 293.5
### Enter Moses H. Cone Memorial Park

### 294.0
### Cone Manor House (Flat Top Manor) and Craft Center
Flat Top Manor, the summer home built by the wealthy textile magnate Moses H. Cone, now serves as a visitor information center, including a regionally focused bookstore. The Southern Highland Craft Guild presents exhibitions and crafting demonstrations in addition to its retail shop. Wheelchair-accessible public restrooms are reached by a gracefully curving path approximately 100 yards from the manor. Signs provide information on Moses H. Cone Memorial Park and on the nearby Figure 8 Trail.

Facilities on the Parkway continue to be contracted out by the park service. With the exception of visitor centers, all of the business establishments along the Parkway's 469-mile length are private enterprises.

Since the first modest sandwich shop opened, the Parkway has expanded its tradition of service-oriented facilities to cover most of the Parkway's length. Today several companies work with the park service to provide gas stations, restaurants, lodging, gift shops, and other services.

At Glendale Springs, the Northwest Trading Post (milepost 258.7), which also opened in 1951, was established by a local group, sponsored by the Northwest North Carolina Development Corporation. The Trading Post features regional folk crafts and treats from local kitchens.

The estate included Flat Top Mountain and Rich Mountain, landscaped extensively with maple, hemlock, and white pine. The 23-room mansion was exquisite, filled with art and objects from Asia. Most of the furnishings and lumber were hauled by oxen from Lenoir. The Cones were almost self-sufficient, with their own dairy, vegetable gardens, carbide gas plant, and local employees.

The estate includes some 25 miles of beautiful carriage paths that are popular with horseback riders, hikers, runners, and cross-country skiers. These trails can be accessed directly from the manor house and from Bass Lake. Nearby, privately owned stables offer horseback rides.

Trails

Hiking is probably the best way to get a feel for the estate. Rich Mountain Trail (4.3 miles, moderate), the longest and least used trail on the estate, leads to the summit of Rich Mountain and offers views of the manor and the grounds. Flat Top Mountain Trail (3 miles, moderate) climbs to the Cones' cemetery and an observation tower that affords a 360-degree view. Watkin Road (3.3 miles, moderate) is known for an exceptional variety of wildflowers in the spring. Bass Lake Road (1 mile, easy) circles Bass Lake. The Maze (2.3 miles, moderate) twists and turns through thick forest. Duncan Road (2.5 miles, moderate) passes by stands of white pines planted by Cone. Black Bottom Road (0.5 miles, easy) travels through moist bottomland forest. Deer Park Road (0.8 miles, easy to moderate) was so named because Cone imported herds of deer and kept them enclosed in "parks." A self-guiding trail, the Figure 8 (0.7 miles, easy) begins behind the manor house. Signs provide information about the Cones and their estate, as well as the flowers along the trail.

Cone made his estate a model of scientific apple growing. He cultivated 29,000 apple trees on his estate, producing 75 varieties of apples and winning several awards at national fairs and international exhibitions. You can see remnants of Flat Top Orchard from the manor's porch. He built two lakes on his estate, including the 36-acre Bass Lake, which you can also see from the porch, and a heart-shaped pool, which is just above Bass Lake.

The Parkway Craft Center is operated by the Southern Highland Craft Guild, an association dedicated to promoting and preserving traditional and contemporary crafts. The center houses many crafts, including pottery and paintings, hooked rugs and hand-woven items, basketry, glassware, and sculpture. Members of the guild hold craft demonstrations on the manor's porch during the summer.

## 294.6
### US 221

Two miles to Blowing Rock; 17 miles to Linville. Exit here and follow Shulls Mill Road under the Parkway to reach Trout Lake, another of Moses Cone's creations. Trout Lake Trail (1-mile loop, easy) circles the lake and is popular with joggers.

## 295.3
### Sims Creek Overlook

A house owned by a man named Hamp Sims once stood nearby. It is said that this odd old fellow used to sleep in a coffin made to his own specifications, and that he enjoyed scaring visitors who stopped by.

## 295.9
### Sims Pond Overlook

An exhibit here describes the trail system in Julian Price Memorial Park. Access some of those trails here.

## 296.4
### Price Park Picnic Area

Price Park consists of 4,200 acres of mountain land surrounding Price Lake. From 1912 to 1930, lumber barons stripped this tract of virgin trees, primarily chestnut, hemlock, and yellow poplar. Today, a hardwood-conifer forest is gradually returning. Jefferson Standard Life Insurance donated the land for Price Park, which has become one of the most popular recreation areas on the Parkway. More than 50 picnic tables and a comfort station are available in the park.

Boone Fork Trail (4.9-mile loop, strenuous) follows Boone Fork, named for Daniel Boone's nephew Jesse, who built a cabin in the area and lived off the land from 1810 to 1817. The loop accesses the 25-foot Boone Fork Falls and crosses Bee Tree Creek more than a dozen times on the way to its headwaters.

## 296.7
### Price Lake Parking Area
Signs provide information on Julian Price Memorial Park and lake-use regulations. Price Lake Loop Trail (2.3-mile loop, moderate) circles 47-acre Price Lake, which is stocked with trout.

## 296.9
### Price Campground
This campground is the largest on the Parkway. Sites on Loop A are located near Price Lake. Several long trails can be reached from the campground.

## 297.2
### Boone Fork Overlook
A short loop road accesses a boat dock, canoe and row-boat rentals, the campground's amphitheater, and an impressive view of Price Lake. This overlook is the northern trailhead of Tanawha Trail.

## 298.6
### Holloway Mountain Road/US 221
Here, you will find a memorial to Rufus Lenoir Gwyn, a landscape architect from the Blowing Rock area who was instrumental in the layout of the Parkway in North Carolina. This small memorial park, which makes a good picnic stop, includes benches and Gwyn Memorial Trail (0.1 mile, easy).

## 299.0
### Cold Prong Pond Overlook
Cold Prong Loop Trail (0.3-mile loop, easy) travels through a meadow that is filled with strawberries in the summer. Tanawha Trail can also be reached via this trail.

### 299.7
#### View of Calloway Peak
Calloway Peak is the highest point on Grandfather Mountain (5,964 feet), otherwise known as Grandfather's nose. Upper Boone Fork Trail (1 mile, easy) heads south along the upper reaches of Boone Fork, passes a lovely stand of birch trees, and ends at the Boone Fork parking area. From this parking area, you can reach Calloway Peak using one of the trails on the privately owned Grandfather Mountain (purchase of permit required).

### 299.9
#### Boone Fork Parking Area
Cross the bridge over Boone Fork just south of this overlook. The parking area accesses nine trails on Grandfather Mountain (purchase of permit required). Go to the entrance station for Grandfather Mountain on US 221, about 1 mile west of milepost 305.1. Tanawha Trail can be accessed here.

### 300.4
#### Green Mountain Overlook
Winter views of Green Mountain below overlook.

The Parkway's famous Linn Cove Viaduct (MP 304.0)

## 301.8
### Pilot Ridge Overlook
Pilot Ridge is located above the Parkway here on Grandfather Mountain. The rocky outcrop is the "pilot."

## 302.1
### View Wilson Creek Valley
This overlook gives you a sense of what the Great Forest of the East must have looked like, offering an incredible wilderness view of nothing but forest.

## 302.4
### Raven Rocks Overlook
Access to Tanawha Trail here. Across the road you can see the ridgelines of Grandfather Mountain to the right and the tower atop Beacon Heights to the left.

## 302.8
### Rough Ridge Parking Area
This parking area accesses a spectacular section of Tanawha Trail; head up the spur, bear left at the intersection, and cross the arched footbridge over a fork of Little Wilson Creek. For the next 0.7 miles, you will be hiking through a unique ecosystem where rare lichens, wildflowers, and grasses grow. The area is considered a combination rocky summit and high-elevation heath bald. From an open rock outcrop, enjoy the 360-degree view of the Grandfather above and the Linn Cove Viaduct. To ensure the survival of this delicate and amazing area, it is essential for hikers to remain on the trail.

## 303.6
### Wilson Creek Overlook
Take the steps down from the overlook, go under the Parkway, and bear right when you intersect the Tanawha. Here you will see an example of the remarkable work of the Tanawha Trail builders—a beautiful wooden arch footbridge, which was placed across Wilson Creek by helicopter.

## 303.9
### Yonahlossee Overlook
In the winter, this pulloff looks down on the Yonahlossee Trail, also knows as US 221. In 1889, at the tail end of the stagecoach days, Hugh MacRae built Yonahlossee Trail, which served as a toll road between Blowing Rock and Linville until the 1920s, when the

Waterfalls are perhaps nature's most captivating wonder. They seem magical, holding all the secrets of the woods. Although it seems simple—falling water—often we are astonished at finding one of these moving spectacles hidden in the folds of the forest.

Mountain streams leave their birthplace, cascading and rushing toward the sea. They are fed by springs and rains as they travel down ancient slopes, following channels carved out years before. Reaching an edge, they fall, creating an enchanting place to become lost in time and space.

Waterfalls take on many shapes and forms. Some are exceptional for the volume of water that passes through them; others, for the tremendous height from which they fall. For some people, waterfalls are simply an excellent place to picnic. For others, waterfalls are the center of all wild places.

Use extreme caution when visiting waterfalls. Visit the falls on established trails only. Do not climb alongside or in waterfalls, as accidents are likely. Here are some waterfalls you can reach from trails that begin at Parkway overlooks:

**White Rock Falls** (milepost 19.9). This is a small-volume falls, but it spills 30 feet into a beautiful gorge on its way to the North Fork of the Tye River. "White rock" refers to the quartz that is so prevalent in the area. Moderate, 1.8 miles round-trip.

**Apple Orchard Falls** (milepost 78.4). This 150-foot falls flows down the west side of Apple Orchard Mountain (elevation 4,225 feet). Hike this national recreation trail to the falls in the late afternoon, timing your return to the trailhead (Sunset Fields) in order to catch the sunset over the mountains. Moderate, 2.4-mile loop.

**Falling Water Cascades** (milepost 83.1). This waterfall is also on a national recreation trail, which was established in 1982. Stone steps lead down to Falling Water Creek, and a footbridge signifies the beginning of the 200-foot cascade. Two dead-end spurs, marked with signs "150 feet to view,"

trail became part of the state highway system. *Yonahlossee* is the Cherokee word for "trail of the black bear." While the last section of the Parkway was being built, US 221 was used as the detour.

### 304.0
### Linn Cove Viaduct

The 1,243-foot-long Linn Cove Viaduct, along with 12 other bridges, ended the winding, 14-mile detour around Grandfather Mountain and marked the official completion of the Blue Ridge Parkway. The "missing link," a 7.5-mile section of the Parkway left unfinished for 20 provide wonderful vantage points for this moderate-volume flume. Moderate, 1.6-mile loop.

**Cascades** (milepost 271.9). A plaque near the top of the Cascades reads: "Water . . . like liquid lace from overhead . . . dashes past to swirl and slide downward in an abandon of spray and foam ripples." This quote is an accurate description because the narrow, 50-foot waterfall rolls and rushes past you rather than falling at your feet. Moderate, 1.2-mile loop.

**Linville Falls** (milepost 316.4). This waterfall has three trails leading to it with a total of five different views. Linville Falls is probably the most famous waterfall along the Blue Ridge Parkway. It is a double cascade with a vanishing act between the two falls—the upper falls, a wide 15-foot shelf; the lower, a thunderous 45-foot drop. Falls Trail: easy, 1.6 miles round-trip. Plunge Basin Trail: moderate, 1 mile round-trip. Gorge Trail: strenuous, 1.4 miles round-trip.

**Crabtree Falls** (milepost 339.5). This waterfall is on Crabtree Creek in Crabtree Meadows—no mystery where this falls got its name. Crabtree Falls plunges 60 feet down a wide, even rock face, and in May, showy, lilylike trillium covers the ground in the small hollow beneath the falls. Moderate, 2.5-mile loop.

**Glassmine Falls** (milepost 361.2). This is a wet-weather falls, which means it will almost disappear during periods of low water. If you can't view Glassmine Falls after a heavy rain, try visiting in the late afternoon. With the sun shining on this 800-foot falls, the wet rock face looks like glass. No hike necessary.

**Waterfalls in Graveyard Fields** (milepost 418.8). A 0.2-mile paved trail leads to a wooden bridge over the Yellowstone Prong of the East Fork of the Pigeon River. The trail left leads to the 50-foot Upper Yellowstone Falls; the trail right, to the 60-foot Second Falls. Upper Yellowstone Falls: easy, 3.2 miles round-trip. Second Falls: moderate, 0.8 miles round-trip.

years because of easement problems and environmental concerns, opened to traffic on September 11, 1987.

The severe damage to the rugged and rocky Linn Cove of Grandfather Mountain that would have been caused by any of the earlier proposals led to years of controversy between Hugh Morton, owner of Grandfather Mountain, and the park service. Governor Dan K. Moore finally negotiated a compromise—an elevated roadway, an S-curve skirting the perimeter of the mountain. The viaduct became the most complex segmented concrete bridge in the world—at a cost of $10 million.

Figg and Muller Engineers, Inc., created the method

of construction for the viaduct, which includes most every type of alignment geometry used in building highways. The design required connecting 153 precast sections that were built off the mountain and matched to fit the preceding segment. These were lowered by stiff-leg cranes onto seven piers, which were built in succession and from the ground up.

The advanced construction technology eliminated the need for blasting, an access road, and heavy machinery. Vegetation, except directly under the viaduct, was left untouched. Silt fences protected streams from contamination, and the cement was tinted with iron oxide to better harmonize with the natural surroundings.

### 304.4
### Linn Cove Information Center

Be sure to go inside the information center and check out the model of the viaduct. The facility provides information on the viaduct, and a trail leads to views of the underside of the Linn Cove Viaduct (wheelchair-accessible).

Interpretive area at the visitor center offers books and other Parkway-related items; video selections include *A Bridge from Yesterday to Tomorrow: Construction of the Linn Cove Viaduct.*

### 304.8
### Stack Rock Parking Area

Stack Rock, a freestanding chimney formation, looks as if rocks have been stacked on top of each other. From this overlook, you can see the famous swinging bridge on Grandfather Mountain. Stack Rock Bridge is just north of this overlook. Tanawha Trail can be accessed here.

### 305.1
### US 221

Three miles to Linville; 13 miles to Blowing Rock. Exit here for Grandfather Mountain.

### 305.2
### Beacon Heights Parking Area

View Grandfather Mountain across the Parkway before hiking Beacon Heights Trail (0.2 miles, moderate), which climbs to the 4,200-foot summit of Beacon Heights. At the summit, head left for the best view. This is the southern trailhead for Tanawha Trail, as well as a connector with Mountains-to-Sea Trail.

*at 5,964 feet, Grandfather Mountain is the highest peak in the Blue Ridge Mountain range*

## Grandfather Mountain Overlook

Foliage at this overlook has been cut to frame a view of Grandfather Mountain. Grandfather Mountain, the highest mountain in the Blue Ridge (elevation 5,964 feet), gets its name from the jagged peaks that create a profile of an old man. The best view of Grandfather's profile is from NC 105 near Foscoe. From the summit, on a clear day, you can see over 100 miles. This mountain resisted erosion because it consists mainly of quartzite, one of the most durable rock types. Grandfather Mountain is one of the oldest mountains in the world.

The mountain is a 4,000-acre wilderness preserve and a designated International Biosphere Reserve. At this privately owned park, you can visit the Mile-High Swinging Bridge that stretches 228 feet between two peaks (two features of Grandfather's face) and an environmental habitat with bears, deer, eagles, and cougars. The nature museum includes a gift shop, restaurant, and movie theater, plus two dozen exhibits on mountain plants, wildlife, and minerals. This park is open year-round, and an entrance fee is charged. To visit Grandfather Mountain, exit onto US 221 (milepost 305.1). For more information, visit www.grandfather mountain.com.

On the Linn Cove Viaduct trails (MP 304.4)

### 307.4
### Grandmother Mountain Parking Area

This overlook sits on the western slope of Grandmother Mountain. You can see the mountain from several places along the Parkway—look for the tower with the blinking light.

### 307.6
### Unnamed Parking Area

This small pulloff offers a nice view of Linville Valley.

### 308.3
### Flat Rock Parking Area

Flat Rock Trail (0.6-mile loop, moderate), a self-guiding trail, is lined with signs identifying much of the flora and fauna and geology in the Blue Ridge. Flat Rock, a quartzite outcrop on the west side of Grandfather, permits

Linville Falls (MP 316.4)

wonderful views to the west. Just south of this overlook, begin travel through Pisgah National Forest for the next 45 miles. A couple of picnic tables are available here.

## 310.0
### Lost Cove Cliffs Parking Area
This overlook is one of several places where people have seen the renowned Brown Mountain Lights (although you can't see Brown Mountain from here). The lights appear to weave in and out of the trees until they reach the edge of the river, then they disappear only to reappear in another spot.

The USGS investigated, discarding the moonshine-still theory. The researchers concluded that there are not enough stills to produce lights in the number and regularity of those seen at Brown Mountain. The USGS then advanced the theory that the lights were caused by the spontaneous combustion of marsh gases, though no marshes are in the area. All these debunked theories leave three older stories to be disproved. As one Native American story goes, the Cherokee and Catawba tribes battled beneath Brown Mountain. The lights are said to be caused by the torches of the maidens who were killed while searching for the Cherokee warriors who fell there in battle. A second, newer, theory was recorded in a Scotty Wiseman bluegrass song about the lights, which claims it is the lantern of a slave who died while searching for his master, who had been injured in a hunting accident. Finally, there is the story about a little girl who went missing during the winter. Her father searched for her until he died, and to this day, his search continues.

A picnic table is available at this overlook.

"
*Linville Gorge offers many recreational opportunities, including hiking, rock climbing, and white-water boating*
"

## 312.2
### NC 181
Two miles to Pineola; 32 miles to Morganton.

## 315.6 🏞
### Camp Creek Overlook
Camp Creek Trail (0.1 mile, easy) arrives at Camp Creek, which flows into the Linville River. The creek, a favorite with local fishermen, was named for the Camp brothers of Chicago, who logged the area in the early 1900s.

## 316.4 🏞 ⛺ 🏞
### Linville Falls Spur Road
At 0.4 miles, pull into River Bend, a one-way loop

located on the Linville River. To locate River Bend Trail (0.1 mile, easy), walk down (left) the spur road, cross the bridge, and turn left into the woods at the sign with the hiker's symbol. This seldom-used trail travels through a rhododendron thicket and reaches a high overlook where you can view the river below.

At 0.5 miles, locate a park service campground that sits on the banks of the Linville River. This is the Parkway's smallest and most popular campground.

At 1.4 miles, reach Linville Falls Visitor Center. Hosting 350,000 visitors annually, Linville Falls is probably the most famous waterfall in the Blue Ridge. The river used to flow straight over the top, but a flood cracked the rock, creating the chute in which the river now flows, cutting the height of the lower falls in half.

The headwaters of Linville River are located on Grandfather Mountain; the river flows to the Catawba Valley through one of the most rugged gorges in the country. The 1,500-foot cliffs of Linville Mountain (west) and Jonas Ridge (east) confine the water for 12 miles while it descends 2,000 feet.

The Cherokee called the area Eeseeoh, which means "river of cliffs." Settlers called the river and the falls Linville to honor explorer William Linville, who in 1766 was attacked and killed in the gorge by natives.

The interpretive area at Linville Falls focuses on family outdoor recreation. A large map details the trails in the area. See pages 90–91 for more information about the three trails to the falls.

On Duggers Creek Trail (0.3-mile loop, easy), nature writers such as John Muir meet you in the woods with thoughtful words of inspiration inscribed on metal plaques. Duggers Creek Falls, one of the smallest named falls in the Blue Ridge, spills over a 10-foot ledge into a miniature canyon.

### 316.5 Linville River Picnic Area

Linville River Bridge Trail (0.1 mile, easy) reaches the Linville River in about 500 feet and then continues to the base of the largest arched bridge on the Parkway, spanning the river in four sections. A work camp set up in the community of Linville Falls built the stone structure circa 1940. Here, you are just a few miles upstream of the Linville Gorge. This overlook makes a wonderful picnic stop and includes a comfort station.

*"apple trees along the Parkway often indicate the former site of a family homestead"*

## 316.6
### Linville River Bridge
The only triple arch bridge on the Parkway is this bridge spanning the Linville River.

## 317.5
### US 221
One mile to the community of Linville Falls; 24 miles to Marion.

## 318.4
### View of North Toe River Valley
Toe River, originally known as Estatoe, was named for a legendary Cherokee maiden.

## 320.8
### Chestoa View Parking Area
There is a 0.1-mile paved and stone path from the

**View from Chestoa View Trail (MP 320.8)**

The 26 tunnels on the Parkway were cut through a total of 2¼ miles of solid rock. They range in length from the 150-foot-long Rough Ridge Tunnel (milepost 349.0) to the 1,434-foot-long Pine Mountain Tunnel (milepost 399.1).

For the first 30 years of Parkway construction, the tunnels were built by drilling blasting holes using a sledgehammer and bit. Drillers would stand on a platform on the back of a truck and slam 10-foot-deep holes into the rock. A circular pattern of diagonal holes were created in the middle of the tunnel and blasted out to create a space for later blasts to fall into. The drilling and blasting would work on areas 10 feet into the rock. After clearing out the rock and shoring up the side of the tunnel, the workers would back the platform up to the rock and begin drilling again to work their way through the mountain. By the 1960s, air hammers and drills were used to make the blasting holes.

parking lot to an impressive view from a stone overlook platform on the edge of a cliff. Tablerock Mountain can be seen to the right, though from this angle, the flat-top profile for which it is known is not as clear as it is from other viewpoints. Between the parking area and that viewpoint, a gravel trail forks off to the right. This is Chestoa View Trail, which leads 0.6 miles out to several more good views.

### 323.0
### Bear Den Overlook
This side of Humpback Mountain once sheltered a bear's den, offering protection from both weather and hunters. Though bears have lost much of their former habitat, first to hunters and later to development, bear den and bear wallow remain names attached to numerous geographic features in the Appalachians.

### 325.9
### Heffner Gap Overlook
Apple trees seen along the Parkway often indicate the site of an old homestead, where the apples would be used to make apple butter, apple pie, and more. The gap is named for Amanda Heffner, who lived here during the mid-1800s.

### 327.3
### View North Cove Valley
This overlook has an interpretive sign on the Crest of

the Blue Ridge Highway. A precursor to today's Parkway, the highway was the idea of Joseph Hyde Pratt at the turn of the 20th century. In 1912, his Appalachian Highway Company began construction of the proposed toll road. Work was halted by World War I with only 8 miles completed. A map of the proposed route of the highway is on the sign. The plan was to connect Tallulah Falls, Georgia, and Marion, Virginia, with a 350-mile road following the ridgetop and to build a chain of motels along the highway.

## 327.5
### McKinney Gap—Altapass Road
Spruce Pine, North Carolina, is 5 miles west, and US 221 is 10 miles east of the gap. The gap is named for Charles McKinney, who lived nearby in the early 1800s with four wives and their 42 children. He had a separate cabin for each of his wives.

## 328.6
### The Loops
An incredible engineering accomplishment in its day, The Loops is the name given to the 29 miles of railroad track built by the Carolina, Clinchfield, and Ohio Railway to bring coal from Kentucky through McKinney Gap to the Carolinas. The track wound back and forth down the mountain, passing through 18 tunnels and descending 1,350 feet in elevation covering just 12 miles as the crow flies.

Begun in 1905, this section of railroad leading up to Spruce Pine was expensive in both dollars and lives. One section cost $1 million for a mile of track. More than 4,000 laborers and 200 mules were working at one time in the nine work camps.

Construction accidents took quite a toll, and when the rail line was first opened, numerous graves lined the tracks between Spruce Pine and Marion. Though no accurate statistics remain, one bloody day is remembered when a 30-foot cutback caved in, burying seven men alive. Later that day nine workers were killed when 1,500 pounds of dynamite were accidentally set off. A worker on the crew, seen earlier that day using a rock to knock the tops off the heavy wood cases holding dynamite, was believed to have caused the second accident.

Fights among the workers also left more than their share of graves along the tracks. Italian, German, and Russian immigrants were recruited to live in the tar-paper shacks along the work site. One well-documented case was the execution of an Italian-born cook, who had been hired by 15 of his fellow immigrants to serve as their camp cook (workers had to buy and cook their own meals). After a tough day of work, they returned to find the cook drunk and no meal prepared. He was tried and sentenced to be tied to a tree and shot. The execution took place promptly. Four of the five immigrants involved were later tried and convicted of murder.

The laborers were paid $1 per 10-hour day for their work. According to the recollections of a laborer from that time, $1 would buy 25 pounds of cornmeal, two pounds of coffee, two pounds of ham, or enough calico to make a baby a dress.

### 329.4
### Swafford Gap
This gap is the namesake of Marcus Swafford (1856–1943), who farmed here.

### 329.8
### View Tablerock Mountain
Tablerock Mountain, at an elevation of 3,909 feet, is 9 miles to the east from this viewpoint.

> *"*
> *a group of Revolutionary soldiers passed through Gillespie Gap on their way to defeat British forces at Kings Mountain, South Carolina*
> *"*

### 330.9
### Gillespie Gap—NC 226
Drive west 4 miles to Spruce Pine, North Carolina, and 4 miles east on NC 226A to Little Switzerland, North Carolina, or 14 miles on NC 226 to Marion, North Carolina. The gap is named for Henry Gillespie, who lived here in the late 1700s.

### Museum of North Carolina Minerals
This museum houses outstanding specimens of the rarest minerals in the state. The emphasis in the museum is the day-to-day uses of the minerals produced in area mines. Nearby Spruce Pine, North Carolina, is the world's leading producer of feldspar, which is used in making fine ceramics. Other important displays in the museum feature quartz, kaolin, and mica. The National Park Service Information Center here includes an interpretive area with a focus on these mineralogical themes. In 2002, the museum underwent a million-dollar renovation and new exhibits were added. One can now find explanations of geological processes, the Linville Falls fault line, and more. For information, call (336) 721-0260 or see www.brpfoundation.org.

The Mitchell County Chamber of Commerce has an office in the museum, and the staff is very knowledgeable about nearby attractions and accommodations. The museum is across the road from the base of the exit ramp in Gillespie Gap.

### Overmountain Victory Trail

In 1780, Major Patrick Ferguson, a leader of the British forces in the south, sought to quickly crush the rebellious colonials with a show of force. Ferguson sent word to American Colonel Isaac Shelby that if the rebellion did not cease, the British Army would march over the mountains (into what is now Tennessee) to "hang their leaders, and lay waste to the country with fire and sword."

Shelby contacted fellow Revolutionary leader Jon Sevier in Tennessee, as well as Benjamin Cleveland and William Campbell, who each rallied forces to go on the offensive against the British. On September 29, 1780, Shelby and Sevier led a group of 1,100 soldiers through Gillespie Gap en route to face Ferguson.

The determined revolutionaries met with forces from Virginia and the Carolinas at the base of the mountains. They marched on, meeting their British opposition at Kings Mountain, South Carolina, where they won a crucial victory. Major Ferguson was killed in the battle. The important victory by the group, remembered as the Overmountain Men for their march to the battle, was one of a series of events leading to the British surrender at Yorktown a year later. This gap is on the Overmountain Victory National Historic Trail, which follows, largely by road, the route of the colonial forces.

### 332.6
### Lynn Gap

A large lynn, or basswood tree, that grew in this gap on the McDowell and Mitchell county line was often used as a wedding canopy by eloping couples.

### 333.4
### Little Switzerland Tunnel

This 542-foot tunnel is the northernmost of the 26 tunnels on the Parkway in North Carolina. The town of Little Switzerland was founded by Heriot Clarkson (1863–1942) and named for its resemblance to the Jura Mountains of Switzerland.

Fraser-fir forests once dominated the summits of the Black Mountains and the Pisgah Range in western North Carolina. Seeds distributed during the ice ages germinated and created unusual Canadian-like forests in the southern Appalachians. These relics of "northern" forests in the South consist of two main trees: red spruce and Fraser fir. Suited to the harsh climate at high elevations, these two evergreens endure on the summits of the tallest mountains in the Blue Ridge, the Blacks and the Pisgah range. Over the last 30 years, the growth rate of these stands has steadily declined. One by one, the fir trees become rust-colored, lose their needles, and finally fall to the forest floor. The major cause? Acid rain–stressed trees falling prey to an insect slightly smaller than a flea.

The balsam woolly adelgid attacks mature fir trees that are 15 to 20 years old. Inserting its mouth part into the tree's bark, the aphidlike insect feeds on fluids from the conductive tissues and injects the tree with a poisonous substance contained in its saliva. This interrupts the tree's ability to circulate water and essential nutrients and stimulates growth abnormalities, causing "gouting" of the buds or twig nodes, and some twigs and branches die back. Most diseased trees eventually die. Once heavily infested, a fir dies within two years.

Unintentionally brought from Europe in 1900, the balsam woolly adelgid, which began its destruction in Canada, had reached Mount Mitchell by the mid-1950s. Today, almost every stand of Fraser fir in the Appalachians has fallen prey to this pest.

### 333.9
### McCall Gap—NC 226A

The town of Little Switzerland is on NC 226A on the east side of the Parkway.

### 336.8

### Wildacres Tunnel

This tunnel is named for the Wildacres Retreat, located nearby and created by Thomas Dixon (1864–1946) in the 1920s. The retreat is now operated by the nonprofit Blumenthal Foundation.

### 337.2
### Deer Lick Gap Overlook

Mineral salts attract deer, who lick the rocks to add needed salt to their diet. These deer licks were well known to hunters who would stake out gaps such as this one searching for game.

An interpretive sign on groundhogs, frequently

Driving the Parkway south of Mount Pisgah, you can't miss the stark evidence of the adelgid's presence, as much of this area is a forest of dead trees. The adelgid's handiwork is especially evident at Richland Balsam Overlook (milepost 431.4), where a self-guided loop trail, complete with an accompanying leaflet, interprets the plight of this special forest.

The adelgid's activity is also readily evident on Mount Mitchell (milepost 355.3). In the mid-1800s, when Dr. Elisha Mitchell explored the Black Mountains and proclaimed Mount Mitchell the highest peak in the East, the mountain's summit harbored an extraordinary stand of Fraser firs.

If the sight of these dying giants alarms you, it's with good reason. In some areas, 80 percent of the trees have been affected. Even worse, the fir has no natural protection, and the adelgid, at least on this continent, has no serious predator. Imported enemies have had little effect, and sprays such as lindane (which carry their own environmental and human health risks) work but require an expensive tree-by-tree application.

Despite appearances, all may not be lost. As researchers continue to study the struggle between the adelgid and the Fraser fir, some optimists note that the adelgid doesn't attack young trees, and in some areas, segments of Fraser-fir forests survive. What happens to the forest in these cases? Seedlings flourish and some old trees resist. This leads some to believe that the Fraser fir is developing genetic resistance and may survive after all.

known as woodchucks or "whistle pigs," tells about the Parkway's most seen animal. They can be seen eating or scurrying away in the grass alongside the Parkway. Early settlers to the area commonly ate groundhogs. A picnic table is available here.

## 338.8
### Three Knobs Overlook
Rising from the ridge in the foreground are the high peaks of the Black Mountain range.

## 339.5
### Crabtree Meadows
You will find a campground, a restaurant, and a gift shop at Crabtree Meadows. The brilliant display of pink crabtree blossoms each May was once the cornerstone of this area's wildflower display. Though hardly any crab trees are here now, the area still offers an impressive array of wildflowers each spring, particularly along Crabtree Falls Trail.

*"*

*groundhogs were a source of food for many early settlers*

*"*

### Crabtree Falls

Crabtree Falls Loop Trail is a 2.5-mile strenuous hike to the 70-foot-tall falls. In the spring, wildflowers abound on this trail. By July, ferns fill the forest and soak in the spray of the falls, with rosebay rhododendrons in bloom along the trail. The path to the falls is a rugged 0.9 miles, with a gentler 1.5-mile return following Crabtree Creek downstream before looping back to the parking area. The trailhead for this hike is at a parking area in the campground.

### 340.2

### Crabtree Meadows Picnic Area

This picnic area has 82 tables and a restroom.

### 342.2
### Black Mountains Overlook

At this overlook, an interpretive sign on the Black Mountain range features a drawing of the range's profile, pointing out the peaks. The range is the highest in the East, with an average elevation of 6,000 feet.

### 344.1
### Buck Creek Gap

East to Marion, 16 miles; west to Burnsville, 17 miles.

### 344.4
### Twin Tunnels

Only about a quarter of a mile apart, the twin tunnels are not actually twins in length. The northernmost tunnel is the shorter twin at 300 feet; the southernmost is 401 feet long.

### 345.3
### Singecat Ridge Overlook

The view here is actually of Onion Knob (to the left) and Mackey Mountain (to the right). Lake Tahoma is in the center, and Singecat Ridge is mostly hidden behind Onion Knob. The origin of its name has been lost to time.

There is access to the Mountains-to-Sea Trail here. For the next hundred miles or so, the Parkway offers continual access to this long-distance trail.

### 347.6
### Big Laurel Gap—USFS Road Crossing (gravel)

USFS 482 descends east to Black Mountain Campground, managed by the forest service in the Curtis

Creek area of Pisgah National Forest. The elevation here is 4,048 feet. Big Laurel refers to the rosebay rhododendron, the largest of the rhododendrons growing along the Parkway.

## 349.0
### Rough Ridge Tunnel

This 150-foot tunnel is the shortest of the 26 tunnels on the Parkway.

## 349.2
### Licklog Ridge Overlook

At 4,602 feet, this overlook offers a view of Grandfather Mountain, Linville Mountain, Woods Mountain, Mackey Mountain, and Chestnutwood Mountain. Licklog Ridge is to the right and was named for the lick-log, a log notched to hold salt for cattle. Domesticated farm animals such as cattle and sheep once lived off the land below.

## 349.9
### Mount Mitchell Overlook

At 6,684 feet above sea level, Mount Mitchell is the highest mountain in the east. The elevation at this viewpoint is a respectable 4,825 feet. The mountain itself is reached from NC 128 at mile 355.3 of the Parkway.

## 350.4
### Green Knob Overlook

This is where the Lost Cove Ridge Trail (also called Green Knob Trail) begins. The forest service trail is 3.1 miles, but it is only half a mile to Green Knob (elevation 5,070), which features a lookout tower. The Snooks Nose trailhead is also here but more difficult to find. The 3.8-mile trail descends to the Curtis Creek Campground to the east of the Parkway.

## 351.9
### Deep Gap—USFS Road (gravel)

Go 5 miles west on this road to reach the forest service's Black Mountain Campground. NC 80 is another 3 miles beyond the campground. The 0.2-mile Deep Gap Trail starts at this gap. The elevation here is 4,284 feet.

## 354.8
### Toe River Gap

The elevation is 5,158 feet here. In the valley below is the confluence of the North and South Toe rivers for

Rhododendrons have quite a reputation in the Blue Ridge Mountains. Like the colors of autumn, their blooms draw thousands of visitors to the Parkway. In late spring and early summer, rhododendrons, joined by flame azaleas and mountain laurels, create a spectacular pink-and-purple procession of flowers.

Three types of rhododendrons grow along the Parkway: Catawba, rosebay, and Carolina. These three evergreen shrubs are members of the family *Ericaceae* (heath family). Locals often refer to rhododendron thickets as "hells" because their tangled trunks and twigs become impassable obstacles in the woods. Landscapers consider the plants popular ornamental bushes because of their showy flowers and large shiny leaves.

While peak bloom depends on elevation, in general the Carolina bloom first, then the Catawba, and finally, the rosebay. Rosebay is the largest of the shrubs; the Carolina is a miniature Catawba, with bloom clusters about half the size.

The three types of rhododendrons have a similar arrangement for pollination but produce flowers of slightly different colors. When there are no blooms, you can identify them by leaf shape. Rosebay has a more streamlined leaf tapering into the stem, and Carolina has the smallest leaves.

Although rhododendrons bloom along the entire length of the Parkway, the area around Craggy Gardens (milepost 364.5) hosts spring's most dazzling flower pageant. Catawba rhododendrons grow in abundance on the slopes and summits at Craggy Gardens, which consists primarily of heath and

which the gap is named. The rivers' names were derived from Estatoe, the name of a Native American princess who drowned herself in the river when her lover was killed by her kinsmen.

### 355.0
### Bald Knob Ridge Trail

There is access to the trail here. The trail leads 2.8 miles to USFS 472.

### 355.3
### Black Mountain Gap—Ridge Junction Overlook

This is where the Parkway leaves the Blue Ridge Mountains to skirt the Black Mountains and pass through the Great Craggies, Pisgah Ledge, and the Great Balsams before reaching the Smokies. The elevation is 5,160 feet. This gap was first called Beech Gap, then Swannanoa Gap, before being called Black Mountain Gap grassy balds. In June, the low-growing vegetation of the balds yields an unobstructed view of acre upon acre of rhododendrons—an unbroken carpet of color.

## Catawba rhododendron
> Scientific name: *Rhododendron catawbiense*
> Local name: Purple laurel
> Bloom date: Mid-May to late June
> Color: Pink to purple blooms
> Location: Abundant along the Parkway
> Special note: Most common

## Rosebay rhododendron
> Scientific name: *Rhododendron maximum*
> Local name: White rhododendron or big laurel
> Bloom date: June to early August
> Color: Pale pink to white
> Location: Deep forests and wet places such as stream banks
> Special note: State flower of West Virginia

## Carolina rhododendron
> Scientific name: *Rhododendron minus*
> Local name: Punctatum
> Bloom date: Late April to June
> Color: Pale lilac or rose pink
> Location: Rocky outcrops such as the cliffs of Linville Gorge
> Special note: Least common on the Parkway

since 1949. Views of the Black Mountains and the South Toe Valley.

### Boundary Asheville Watershed
Southbound drivers note that for the next 15 miles, parking is permitted only at overlooks. For more information on the watershed, see milepost 363.4.

### Mount Mitchell
NC 128 leads 4.8 miles to Mount Mitchell, the highest point east of the Mississippi at 6,684 feet. Mitchell is part of the Black Mountain range, which boasts 6 of the 10 highest points in the East, all within a 15-mile range.

Mount Mitchell was named for Dr. Elisha Mitchell, who was the first to measure the height of the Black Mountains. Although nearby Grandfather Mountain was presumed to be the highest mountain at the time, Mitchell felt sure that the Black Mountains were higher. In 1835, using barometric pressure readings, Mitchell calculated the height of the peaks in the Black Mountain range. He judged Big Black (now known as Mount Mitchell) to be the highest at 6,476 feet. The summit was quickly named in his honor and was listed in *Smith's Geography and Atlas* of 1839 as the highest peak in the East.

In 1844, Mitchell remeasured his peak and calculated it to be 6,672 feet—only 12 feet off the actual elevation. In the 1850s, Thomas Clingman, a former student of Mitchell, contested Mitchell's claim. Clingman, a U.S. senator from North Carolina, was pushing what was then known as Mitchell Mountain, another summit in the Black Mountain range, as being the highest peak in the area. Clingman claimed that Mitchell Mountain, now known as Clingman's Peak, was 6,941 feet tall. A battle was waged through competing North Carolina newspapers as to whose peak was the highest—Mitchell's or Clingman's.

As supporters took sides in the growing debate, Mitchell, now in his 60s, returned to the Black Mountains to verify and refine his measurements. On June 27, 1857, Mitchell fell to his death from a 40-foot waterfall. It was 8:19 p.m., as evidenced by his watch, which was broken in the fall. It has since been proved that Mount Mitchell is 6,684 feet tall. It was eventually determined that Clingman's Peak is 6,499 feet in elevation, a difference of 185 feet. Clingmans Dome, on the other hand, which is located in the Great Smoky Mountains National Park, is the second-highest peak east of the Mississippi River, standing at 6,643 feet in elevation, only 41 feet shorter than Mount Mitchell. Although originally buried in Asheville, Mitchell's remains were later moved to the summit of Mount Mitchell.

### Mount Mitchell State Park

Mount Mitchell was established as North Carolina's first state park in 1915. The park now offers a nine-site family campground with one comfort station. Hikers may also backpack along the several trails in the park. Trail shelters are available for overnight use. A picnic area with 40 tables, grills, and drinking water is located near the summit. Two picnic shelters with stone fireplaces can be used for larger gatherings. Also atop Mount Mitchell are an observation tower, a museum, a concession stand, and a restaurant—all open in-season only.

Trails in Mount Mitchell State Park include Old

Mitchell Trail (2 miles, moderate); Mount Mitchell Trail (6 miles, strenuous), which leads from the summit of Mitchell to the Black Mountain Campground; Balsam Trail (0.75 miles, easy), which is a self-guided nature trail; Camp Alice Trail (0.75 mile, strenuous); and Deep Gap Trail (6 miles, moderate). Mountains-to-Sea Trail can be reached via the access road.

## 358.5
### Highest Point on the Parkway North of Asheville
The elevation here is 5,676 feet.

## 359.8
### Balsam Gap Overlook
You may access Big Butt Trail (6 miles, strenuous) here. Mountains-to-Sea Trail can also be accessed here. Balsam Gap is where the Black Mountains and the Great Craggy Mountains join. This gap is the site of an old lumber railway that operated near the turn of the 20th century. The elevation here is 5,317 feet.

## 361.1
### Cotton Tree Gap
This gap was named for the pale-green lichen, or cotton moss, that grows on nearby trees; elevation is 5,141 feet.

## 361.2
### View Glassmine Falls
View the 800-foot falls here. Stroll up the 0.1-mile paved path to a bench and different view of the falls, which pour over the exposed rock face of Horse Range Ridge. At the base of the falls are the remains of the old Abernathy Mine, a mica mine that operated at the turn of the 20th century, and the site of a mica miner's cabin. Mica is also known as isinglass, and by the locals as glass, thus the name Glassmine Falls. You can access Mountains-to-Sea Trail here.

## 363.4
### Bullhead Gap—View Graybeard Mountain
At an elevation of 5,365 feet, Graybeard Mountain has been a weather predictor to the people of the valley below it for centuries. When the summit is "bearded" by gray clouds, the people say that rain is in the forecast. This overlook is located at Peach Orchard Glade, which is made up of 200-year-old yellow birch, beech, and yellow buckeye.

The Mountains-to-Sea Trail crosses here. An exhibit on the Asheville Watershed describes the 20,000-acre area that is one of the largest city-owned watersheds in the United States. This watershed supplies 30 million gallons of water daily and also protects one of the few remaining spruce-fir forests in the area. Within the Asheville Watershed, which runs from milepost 355.3 to 370.3, parking is permitted only at overlooks, and hiking is allowed only in designated areas to avoid contaminating the water supply.

### 364.1

### View Craggy Dome

In this parking area, an exhibit tells about the Catawba rhododendron. During mid-June, depending on the weather, the rhododendrons at Craggy Dome (elevation 6,085 feet) and Craggy Gardens color the area with their beautiful purple blossoms. Those bearing white blossoms are called rosebay rhododendrons.

The Craggy Dome area is also the access point for Craggy Pinnacle Trail, which leads 0.7 miles to the summit of Craggy Pinnacle, a good spot to watch the annual hawk migration. The plant life in this area—rhododendrons, gnarled sweet birches, and blueberries—is part of a very fragile habitat left over from the last ice age. In fact, the University of Georgia identified a minimum of six rare, endangered, and threatened plants on the pinnacle

Rhododendrons in bloom at Craggy Gardens (MP 364.1)

alone. The park is working to protect the area. It is important that you remain on the designated trail.

Craggy Gardens got its name from the Great Craggy Mountains, so called because of the rock outcrops on the mountain summits. The abundance of flowering shrubs (rhododendrons, azaleas, and mountain laurels) and wildflowers gave the impression of a large garden.

## 364.4

### Craggy Pinnacle Tunnel
The pinnacle reaches an elevation of nearly 6,000 feet and was once known as Buckner's Knob. The tunnel is 245 feet in length.

*" rhododendron flowers at Craggy Gardens reach their peak sometime between mid- to late June "*

## 364.5

### Craggy Gardens Visitor Center and Parking Area
The visitor center offers information and restrooms. The interpretive area here features a large selection of items geared to nature study and outdoor recreation. The visitor center is also the access point for the self-guided Craggy Gardens Trail. This 0.8-mile trail leads 0.3 miles to a shelter, where the self-guided portion ends. The shelter was built of American chestnut by the Civilian Conservation Corps in 1936 before this section of the Parkway was constructed. The next half mile descends to the Craggy Gardens picnic area. Halfway between the shelter and the picnic area is a short loop trail that leads to a gazebo overlooking the valley below. An exhibit at the visitor center parking lot provides information on Craggy Gardens Trail, which takes you through a high mountain rhododendron bald.

## 365.5

### Craggy Flats Tunnel
This tunnel is 400 feet in length.

## 367.6

### Bee Tree Gap—Craggy Gardens Picnic Area
The picnic area, down a short road (right fork), is actually situated in Bear Pen Gap, so named because bear traps were once set in the vicinity. The bears often fed on the livestock that grazed in the gap, and farmers trapped the bears to stop the predation. The picnic area has 86 sites, 2 wheelchair-accessible sites, 3 water fountains, and 2 comfort stations. One comfort station is wheelchair-accessible.

Craggy Knob here reaches an elevation of nearly

5,700 feet. It was once known as Bee Tree Mountain or High Top of Bee Tree (bee trees were so named because bees nested in the tree, producing honey).

## Trails

Craggy Gardens Trail can be accessed from the picnic area and followed back to the visitor center. The Mountains-to-Sea Trail can be reached here as well. From this long-distance trail, you can reach Snowball Mountain Trail and Douglas Falls Trail (also known as Carter Creek Falls Trail). Snowball Mountain Trail is 8 miles round-trip to the summit of Snowball Mountain and back. Douglas Falls Trail can be reached by following Mountains-to-Sea Trail north 1.5 miles to the trail junction. Hike 3 miles along Douglas Falls Trail to the 70-foot Carter Creek Falls. The trail passes by cascades and two virgin hemlock groves.

## 370.3
### Boundary Asheville Watershed

Northbound drivers note that for the next 15 miles, parking is permitted only at overlooks. For more information on the watershed, see milepost 363.4.

## 372.1
### View Lane Pinnacle

In the early 1800s, iron was mined out of the north face of this pinnacle by Charles Lane, who operated an iron forge on Reems Creek in Asheville.

## 373.8
### View Bull Creek Valley

A sign here tells the story of the last buffalo to be seen in the area. Allegedly the last buffalo was killed near the Parkway in 1799 by Joseph Rice. This area was also home to the American elk, or wapiti. The elevation here is 3,483 feet.

## 374.4
### Tanbark Ridge Tunnel

The ridge was the site of an old tannery. This is one of the Parkway's longer tunnels at 780 feet.

## Rattlesnake Lodge

Just after you leave the tunnel, to your right, a half-mile trail leads to the ruins of Rattlesnake Lodge. If interested, you may park on the right-of-way and hike up to the remains of the house—the foundation, a springhouse, and more. The lodge was built by Dr. Chase P. Ambler, founder of the Appalachian National Park Association. Built at the turn of the 20th century (1903–1904) for his family as a summer retreat, the lodge was sold by Ambler in November 1920 after the death of his wife. It burned shortly thereafter. During their first three years in residence, the family killed 41 rattlesnakes in the vicinity of the house, hence the name. It is said that Ambler would pay $5 for the skin of a rattler, which was approximately a week's wages at the time. Ambler used the snakes' skins to "paper" the ceiling of the lodge's living room. At Rattlesnake Lodge, you will also find access to the Mountains-to-Sea Trail.

## 375.4
### Bull Gap
The elevation here is 3,107 feet. Before they disappeared from the East, buffalo used this gap to travel from one valley to the next.

## 376.7
### Tanbark Ridge Overlook
At an elevation of 3,175 feet, this overlook offers a view of the ridge named for the tannery at Tanbark Ridge Tunnel (milepost 374.4). The peaks of High Swan, High Knob, and Lane's Pinnacle can also be seen from here.

## 380.0
### View Haw Creek Valley
Haw Creek was named in 1860 for the black haw bushes growing along its banks. The elevation here is 2,720 feet.

**(On following page)**
**Deer are one of the Parkway's most popular denizens**

# Asheville and Vicinity

• • • • • • • • • • • • • • • • • • • • • • •

The city of Asheville, founded in 1793 and named for jurist Samuel Ashe, has long been a magnet for people looking to get away to the mountains. The city's best-known tourist attraction, Biltmore Estate, is an extreme example of building a mountain house to get away. George Washington Vanderbilt's 255-room French Renaissance chateau, completed in 1895, and its surrounding gardens and winery give a new generation of visitors another reason to get away to the mountains and visit Asheville.

Vanderbilt's initial land purchase was the 86-acre tract south of Asheville on which the estate is built, but he soon owned 125,000 acres, including Mount Pisgah. Vanderbilt hired Gifford Pinchot (and later, Carl A. Schenck) to manage his vast forest lands, which were in sad shape at the time due to fire and overgrazing. These men believed you could cut a forest and still preserve it; their plans and practices were the beginning of scientific forestry and natural resource conservation in the United States (see Cradle of Forestry Overlook at milepost 411.0).

In 1914, after Vanderbilt's death, his heirs sold 86,700 acres of the land (including Mount Pisgah) to the United

When hiking trails along the Parkway in North Carolina, you may run across the circular white blazes of the Mountains-to-Sea Trail (MST). Proposed as a connection between the western mountain country and the seashore of North Carolina, MST, when completed, will be the state's longest trail at 1,000 miles. At this point, more than 500 miles of footpath exist, with temporary connections on back roads and state routes that allow one to hike across the entire state.

The idea is to put existing public land to use, extending a corridor across the state, and to create a "trunk" trail that links major population centers with the state's natural resources—national forests, national and state parks, city and county parks (including greenways), and rivers. As proposed, the western trailhead is on top of Clingman's Dome in the Great Smoky Mountains National Park, and the eastern trailhead is at Jockey Ridge State Park on the Outer Banks at Nags Head.

From its western trailhead at Clingman's Dome, MST leaves the Great Smoky Mountains National Park, runs through a piece of the Cherokee Indian Reservation, and then follows the Parkway, for the most part, all the way to Doughton Park (milepost 240.0). Meandering from the motor road at several points, MST travels through the Nantahala and Pisgah national forests (including portions in the East Prong and Shining Rock wilderness areas), the city of Asheville, Mount Mitchell State Park, and Wilson Creek and Linville Gorge areas. MST shares its footpath with several of the Parkway's trails, including Buck Springs Gap, Shut-in, Tanawha, and Boone Fork—plus the carriage trails at the Cone Manor House.

From Doughton Park, MST turns southeast to cross Stone Mountain, Pilot Mountain, Hanging Rock, Eno River, Falls of the Neuse, Cliffs-of-the-Neuse, and Waynesboro State Parks. Plans also include the Croatan National Forest on the Neusiok Trail, a crossing to Ocracoke from Cedar Island, and the 75-mile Cape Hatteras Beach Trail.

MST is primarily the work of volunteers—residents' task forces specifically established to be responsible for segments along the corridor, and other existing organizations throughout the state, such as canoe, hiking, and equestrian clubs. With technical assistance from the park service, the forest service, and the state trails program, volunteers have done everything—which includes design, layout, construction, and maintenance of the trail and any trailside facilities. For additional information about MST, visit the Web site of Friends of the Mountains-to-Sea Trail at www.ncmst.org.

States for use in forest preservation. This land, which is now part of Pisgah National Forest, became the first national forest east of the Mississippi.

Asheville has also long been home to a thriving community of local artists. The Parkway's Folk Art Center, Asheville's Pack Place Arts and Science Center and the Thomas Wolfe House, and Carl Sandburg's Home in Flat Rock are places to immerse yourself in Asheville's artistic past and present. The historic towns of Black Mountain and Old Fort are east of Asheville via I-40. The Mountain Gateway Museum in Old Fort represents rural pioneer life and culture in southern Appalachia.

## 382.0
### Folk Art Center

Opened as a cooperative effort between the National Park Service and the Southern Highland Handicraft Guild, and with the aid of a grant from the Appalachian Regional Commission, the Folk Art Center is the home of the Allanstand Craft Shop. This craft shop is one of Appalachia's best known, and it features the art of more than 700 guild members. The guild was founded in 1930, and the center was dedicated in 1980 on the guild's 50th anniversary.

The 31,000-square-foot center is the base of all the guild's operations. It houses a museum and provides office as well as exhibition and demonstration space. Traditional as well as modern crafts are available in the craft shop, and throughout the year, demonstrations, fairs, competitions, and other celebrations are scheduled at the center. For more information, call (828) 298-7928 or visit www.southernhighlandguild.org.

The National Park Service Information Center here includes an interpretive area focused on Appalachian craft and culture.

## 382.5
### US 70

Drive 5 miles west to downtown Asheville, North Carolina; east, 9 miles, to Black Mountain, North Carolina.

## 383.6
### Swannanoa River

The name is a corruption of Suwali-Nunna, which is Cherokee for "trail of the Suwali tribe."

## 384.1

### Blue Ridge Parkway Visitor Center and Headquarters

The Parkway's newest visitor center is a $9.8-million, ultramodern building built to LEED (Leadership in Energy and Environmental Design) standards. A plant-covered roof, solar-heat collecting walls, radiant floor heating, and computer-controlled energy systems are just some of the ways this visitor center is conserving the resources that are so important to the Blue Ridge Parkway—clear air, water, biologically diverse forests, mountain views, and the agricultural landscape. The center boasts interactive exhibits, touch-screen computer exhibits, large-scale photos, and exhibits that allow you to create your own arch bridge, as well as exhibits on tourism and recreational vehicles, landscape architecture, and much more.

A gift shop and restrooms are also available. The film *The Blue Ridge Parkway—America's Favorite Journey* is shown hourly in a 70-seat theater with surround sound.

## 384.7
US 74

It is 5 miles west to Asheville, North Carolina; a quarter mile to I-40; and 17 miles east to Bat Cave, North Carolina. You can access the Mountains-to-Sea Trail here.

## 388.8
US 25

It is west 5 miles to Asheville, North Carolina; east 16 miles to Hendersonville, North Carolina. You can access the Mountains-to-Sea Trail here.

# High Mountain Wilderness Views

• • • • • • • • • • • • • • • • • • • • • •

The southernmost stretch of the Parkway, between Asheville and the Great Smokies, boasts the highest peaks on the Parkway—Waterrock Knob and Richland Balsam. Here, the Parkway climbs to 6,047 feet, the highest point along the 469-mile motor road, and you will drive at elevations above 4,000 feet, with many miles above 5,000 feet. During the winter, because of the extreme cold at these high elevations, this part of the Parkway is closed more often than the rest of the Parkway.

The classic Parkway postcard scene—ridgeline after ridgeline shrouded with fog—can be found from overlooks along this section. Many overlooks afford extensive views of the Great Smokies, but unfortunately, due to high elevations, the views are often lost in clouds.

This section is wild, traveling along portions of Pisgah and Nantahala national forests for most of its length. Remote, with only a half dozen road crossings in 75 miles, and with towns usually 15 to 25 miles down the mountain, this part of the Parkway is also rugged, located high on a ledge and composed of many rocky cliff faces.

Leaving Asheville and heading south, the Parkway climbs from the French Broad River to traverse three ranges—the

Pisgah Ledge, the Great Balsams, and the Plott Balsams. The last 10 miles run along ridges northwest of the Cherokee Indian Reservation. Reaching the Oconaluftee River, the motor road's southern terminus, the Parkway meets the Great Smoky Mountains National Park.

The long trails in this section are more isolated than other Parkway trails and include the Mountains-to-Sea Trail (MST) and Shut-in Trail. The Parkway also provides access to Pisgah National Forest and Shining Rock Wilderness Area trails.

Shut-in Trail, in Vanderbilt's day, extended from the Biltmore House in Asheville to Buck Springs Hunting Lodge near Mount Pisgah. Because this national recreation trail, first built in the 1890s, was not preserved, volunteers rebuilt original sections and created new sections, bringing Shut-in Trail back to life.

The trail, now part of the MST, runs for 16.3 miles, crisscrossing the Parkway several times, from Bent Creek (milepost 393.6) to Buck Springs Gap Overlook (milepost 407.6). The elevation rises from 2,025 feet at the French Broad River to nearly 5,000 feet at Mount Pisgah. The trail is named for the limited, or shut-in, views along the footpath caused by the dense thickets of rhododendrons.

> **"**
> *this section of the Parkway passes through some of the remotest areas of its 469-mile length*
> **"**

### 393.5
#### French Broad River
This river was called the French Broad to distinguish it from the Broad River. The "French" reflects that the area into which the river drained was French- and Native American–held at the time. The Cherokee had several names for this river, including Tah-kee-os-tee, or "racing waters," as well as Poe-li-co, Agiqua, and Zillicoah. You can access the Mountains-to-Sea Trail here.

### 393.6 
#### NC 191
Nine miles to Asheville; 18 miles to Hendersonville. There is a three-sided wayside exhibit here about the Blue Ridge Parkway. Access to the North Carolina Arboretum is on the exit ramp to NC 191.

#### The North Carolina Arboretum
The arboretum is a member of the National Center for Plant Conservation, a network of 36 public gardens in the United States that participate in conserving rare or endangered plant species. Along with a visitor education center and greenhouse, and 65 acres of formal and naturalized gardens, including a Bonsai Exhibition Garden, the

grounds provide varied opportunities for hiking, biking, walking, and running. Open daily, the arboretum also has a gift shop and restaurant. For additional information, call (828) 665-2492 or visit www.ncarboretum.org.

### 393.8
### View French Broad

The French Broad originates near Rosman, North Carolina, where the north, west, middle, and east forks of the river join. The river flows north and west for 187 miles through North Carolina and into Tennessee to Douglas Lake. Fur traders named the river using the second word to depict its vast width and the first word to distinguish it from another waterway in English territory.

### 396.4
### View Walnut Cove

Here, you will find a grove of walnut trees and a good view of the French Broad River Valley.

### 397.1
### Grassy Knob Tunnel

This tunnel is among the Parkway's longest at 770 feet.

### 397.3
### Sleepy Gap Parking Area

Grassy Knob Trail (0.9 miles, strenuous) descends to Bent

**View from the Blue Ridge Parkway (MP 390.0)**

What is the largest animal in the Blue Ridge? The black bear. Yes, there are bears in these hills! Black bears can live to be 25 years old, grow to a height of five feet, and they weigh, on average, 176 pounds. While they usually carry their bulky bodies at an unhurried saunter, bears can accelerate to a surprising 25 miles per hour if required. In addition to a speedy sprint, most black bears climb trees and swim well. Their keen sense of smell compensates for their mediocre eyesight and poor hearing.

As omnivores, black bears dine on almost everything nature offers. The enormous assortment includes the usual bear fare (fruit and fish, grubs and honey), as well as grasses, mushrooms, roots, ants, frogs, salamanders, mice, chipmunks, and carrion. Their powerful nonretractile claws help them dig, pick, and catch the items on this long menu.

Bears don't hibernate. Instead, they sleep a good deal in the winter and their metabolism remains normal. In true hibernation, body temperature drops significantly and heart rate slows

Creek Experimental Forest, where the forest service studies trees and problems caused by fungi, insects, and diseases.

### 398.3
### View Chestnut Cove

American chestnuts once covered this hill and were the dominant tree in the southern Appalachians. The nuts fed forest animals and farmers' hogs. The wood produced a valuable, rot-resistant timber. Around the turn of the 20th century, an Asian fungus that obstructs a tree's tissues and literally chokes it to death was accidentally introduced in New York and destroyed all chestnuts along its range within 40 years. On occasion, you may see a sprout or young tree, but it will eventually succumb to the fungus.

*"before the chestnut blight, the American chestnut was an important agricultural resource throughout the Southeast"*

### 399.1
### Pine Mountain Tunnel

Measuring 1,434 feet long, Pine Mountain Tunnel is the longest on the Parkway.

### 400.0
### Bad Fork Valley Overlook

At an elevation of 3,350 feet, this overlook offers long-range views of the valley below.

### 400.3
### Bent Creek Gap

Exit here to reach Lake Powhatan, a forest service recreation area where you can swim, fish, picnic, and camp.

to one or two beats per minute. (Parkway animals that truly hibernate include groundhogs, chipmunks, and bats.) During the winter, black bears living in the Blue Ridge Mountains seek out a safe shelter and "nap" for as long as several weeks during the coldest spells.

Black bears have achieved "name fame" status on the Parkway. Overlooks named in honor of the black bear run the length of the Parkway. A concentration of such place names is located along Pisgah Ridge, where bears are most prevalent. In a 3-mile stretch between milepost 427 and 430, discover Bear Pen Gap, Bear Trap Gap, and Beartrail Ridge.

Parkway travelers rarely see bears, though. Unlike many national park campgrounds, the Parkway campgrounds are seldom visited by bears. The black bear, although potentially dangerous, almost never attacks humans. More a nuisance than a real threat, bears seek food and like to feign attacks, which can result in an occasional accident.

## 400.9
### Ferrin Knob Tunnels #1, #2, and #3
Named for the ferns (once referred to locally as ferrins) on their backs. Ferrin Knob Tunnel #1 is the first and longest of these triplet tunnels at 561 feet. Tunnel #2, 421 feet, is at mile 401.3, and Tunnel #3, 375 feet, is at mile 401.5.

## 401.0
### Wash Creek Valley Overlook
Wash Creek is below the overlook; during heavy rains, the creek rises, overflowing its banks and forming a wash.

## 401.9
### Beaver Dam Gap Overlook
Prior to 1900, beavers were plentiful here. Beaver Dam Creek flows north to the French Broad River. A picnic table is here.

## 402.5
### View Stony Bald
At 3,750 feet, take in broad views of the landscape below.

## 403.0
### Young Pisgah Ridge Tunnel
This tunnel is 412 feet in length.

## 403.6
### Big Ridge Overlook
Long-range views. Elevation 3,820 feet.

## 404.0

### Fork Mountain Tunnel

This tunnel is 389 feet in length.

## 404.2

### View Hominy Valley

To make hominy, pioneers soaked corn kernels in weak wood lye until the kernels swelled and the hulls floated to the top, leaving the soft center in edible form.

## 404.5

### Mills River Valley Overlook

Named for William Mills, who lived in this area in the late 1700s and early 1800s. A hunter, Mills reported the last elk to be seen in North Carolina. This is a good spot to watch the annual hawk migration.

## 405.5

### Elk Pasture Gap—NC 151

Candler, 15 miles. Not recommended for trailers and RVs.

## 406.9

### Little Pisgah Tunnel

This tunnel is 576 feet in length.

## 407.3

### Buck Springs Tunnel

This tunnel is 462 feet in length.

## 407.6

### Mount Pisgah

The first parking area on this spur road is Buck Springs Gap Overlook; the second, Mount Pisgah parking area.

### Buck Springs Gap Overlook

Buck Springs Trail (1.1 miles, easy) includes Buck Springs Lodge, George W. Vanderbilt's hunting retreat, and a pedestrian overlook with two benches. Constructed circa 1896, the lodge was built primarily from chestnut logs. The mountain complex, which included a kitchen, dining hall, and several outbuildings, could sleep more than a dozen people. In 1959, North Carolina bought the lodge and surrounding land for construction of the Parkway. Stone walls mark the location of the lodge. Locate the lodge's springhouse in the rhododendrons just to the right, immediately after turning onto the spur road. You can walk inside and see Buck Springs.

### Mount Pisgah Parking Area

While debate exists over who played Moses on this

mountain, there is little doubt that the mountain's name came from a biblical reference. Someone drew a parallel between the land of milk and honey and the extensive view of the French Broad River Valley and what is now Shining Rock Wilderness Area. The name first appeared on record in 1808. Mount Pisgah Trail (1.5 miles, strenuous) gains 712 feet and travels through a northern red oak forest. An observation platform on the summit of Mount Pisgah affords a 360-degree view.

## 407.8

### Mount Pisgah Picnic Area

Picnic Area Loop Trail (0.3-mile loop, easy) provides access to restrooms and picnic sites on a beautiful grassy knoll.

## 408.6

### Mount Pisgah Inn

For generations, Pisgah has been a popular mountain retreat for travelers. The modern facility includes a balcony and private porches offering an incredible mountain view of Pisgah National Forest. The dining room serves breakfast, lunch, and dinner. The complex also houses a gift shop, service station, camp store, and laundromat. Pisgah Inn and its facilities open in late March and operate through November 1. For more information, call (828) 235-8228 or visit www.pisgahinn.com.

Follow Buck Springs Trail (1.1 miles, moderate) to the site of Buck Springs Lodge. The Western Carolina Botanical Club created a leaflet (available at the front desk) for this trail that matches numbered stations and furnishes details about plants such as mayflowers, deerberries, minniebushes, painted trilliums, fetterbushes, goldenrods, and asters. Because the trail travels through a portion of a northern hardwood forest, a remarkable quantity and assortment of plant species exist.

## 408.8

### Mount Pisgah Campground

This campground is the highest and coolest on the Parkway, with the most secluded sites the Parkway has to offer.

The campground is located in Flat Laurel Gap. Because a granite rock base forms a bowl in this gap, there is little runoff and the area remains wet, creating the 85-acre Flat Laurel Gap Bog, which is a rare example of the southern Appalachian bog. At more than 3,000 years, this is the oldest radiocarbon-dated heath community in the southern Appalachians. This plant community is easily damaged by foot travel, so stay on roads and established trails

When the parkway was first established, the views from the roadway were often of cutover forests or farms run down from the loss of topsoil. Through natural reforestation and the conscientious effort by early landscape architects, the Parkway views have improved over the years. Today, more than 1,000 scenic views are offered along the Parkway, including panoramas of surrounding mountains, pastoral and forest views, and views of rivers, streams, and waterfalls.

Still, protecting these viewsheds is an ongoing process. Since the Parkway is a narrow ribbon, usually less than 800 feet in most places, many of the views from the Parkway look over privately held land. Over the years, private and commercial development have changed the views from the Parkway. To limit change, the Parkway works with a number of land

around the campground. The blacktop leading through loop B and C encircles the bog on three sides.

Take Frying Pan Mountain Trail (1.1 miles, strenuous) behind the ranger's cabin to discover a unique form of northern hardwood forest called orchards. Harsh weather in the high mountains twists and retards growth of red oaks and keeps shrubs at a minimum, creating an area that resembles a fruit orchard. At the summit (5,450 feet), a fire tower, still used by Pisgah National Forest, offers beautiful views over Mills and Davidson river valleys.

### 409.3
### View Funnel Top
Wide-range views of Funnel Top Mountain below. The elevation here is 4,925 feet.

### 410.1
### Frying Pan Tunnel
This tunnel is 577 feet in length.

### 410.3
### View Pink Beds
The Pink Beds, a unique upland bog in Pisgah National Forest, extend 5 miles east from the Pisgah Ridge to Soapstone and Dividing Ridge. The "pink" is for the rhododendrons, laurels, and phlox that bloom here.

### 411.0
### Cradle of Forestry Overlook
The Cradle of Forestry was America's first school to

trusts and communities to encourage protection of the views through scenic and conservation easements. When possible, the Parkway also purchases land or advises on development. These efforts protect not only the beauty of the roadway but also the surrounding fields and hillsides.

Many landowners along the Parkway go the extra mile to help perpetuate the historic character of the Parkway landscape. Neighboring farmers still practice the old ways: plowing with mules, stacking cornstalks, and creating haystacks. They even plant "old-style" crops, including tobacco and sorghum. Modern machinery and new crops make these choices unnecessary, but many farmers enjoy sharing older agricultural traditions with visitors.

teach scientific management of forests. In 1895, at a time of heavy logging and few trained foresters, Dr. Carl A. Schenck became the chief forester of the Biltmore Estate. In 1898, he founded the Biltmore Forest School at the base of Mount Pisgah in Vanderbilt's "forest." The first students, many of whom were sons of logging company owners, became the first forest-service employees.

Today, the Cradle of Forestry consists of 6,500 acres designated as a national historic site. A U.S. Forest Service visitor center houses exhibits and a film that illustrate the beginning of scientific forestry, early forestry practices, and natural resource conservation. The Biltmore Campus and Forest Festival Trails, 1-mile paved walkways with self-guided pamphlets, interpret the forestry student's training and a 1908 festival exhibiting the school's achievement. You can also visit a reconstruction of the Biltmore Forest School. To reach the Cradle of Forestry, leave the Parkway at milepost 411.8 and travel 4 miles south on US 276. An entrance fee is charged.

### 411.8
### Wagon Road Gap—US 276
It is 22 miles to Waynesville; 4 miles to the Cradle of Forestry; 18 miles to Brevard.

### 411.9
### View Cold Mountain
Cold Mountain is a 6,030-foot peak made famous by the book by Charles Frazier, and later the movie of the same name, which is about Civil War Appalachia.

If you visit the Parkway on a summer day, you might wonder where the Blue Ridge Mountains are. The beautiful, panoramic shots of blue mountains marching into the distance you saw in the brochure have been replaced by a thick white veil that greatly reduces the visibility. The chief culprit: sulfates produced by the combustion of fossil fuels, namely coal-burning power plants. As a result of this and other pollution sources,

### 412.1
### Wagon Road Gap Parking Area

Wagon Road began life as a footpath and later became a road used by wagons traveling between Brevard and Waynesville. The elevation here is 4,550 feet.

### 413.2
### Pounding Mill Overlook

Enjoy an expansive mountain view that includes Looking Glass Rock. The elevation here is 4,700 feet.

### 415.7
### View Cherry Cove

In September, monarch butterflies from the eastern United States and Canada fly through this narrow gap as they journey toward Mexico. During the mass migration, thousands of butterflies pass by this overlook, although typically a visitor might see 20 to 30 butterflies each hour on a good day. Because of their short life span, other types of butterflies can't attempt such great distances, but monarchs are more like migratory birds, able to fly several thousand miles. Returning in the spring, monarchs lay eggs on milkweed, the only plant they eat.

### 416.2
### Log Hollow Overlook

During the 1880s, loggers cut thousands of trees on the surrounding slopes. Using cant hooks, the loggers would slide the trees down the slopes to the hollow below. Once there, the trees were pulled into the creek bed, dams were opened upstream, and the logs were carried by water downstream to the lumber mill.

### 417.0
### View Looking Glass Rock

This 3,969-foot mountain gets its name from the way the icy or wet rock glitters with reflections of sunlight. Weathering of a larger mountain composed of softer rock—

visibility in the southern Appalachians has declined 80 percent over the last half-century. Air pollution doesn't affect just the views, however; pollution also acidifies streams, hurting fish and other aquatic creatures, and ground-level ozone damages trees and plants. Fortunately, a growing number of individuals and communities are conserving energy at home and at work, paving the way to better views in the future.

quartz, mica, and shale—exposed this granite dome. Looking Glass offers some of the best climbing in the South on its 400-foot sheer face. Elevation is 4,493 feet.

### 418.3
### East Fork Overlook
This is the east fork of the Pigeon River. What you hear is Yellowstone Falls, which is accessed at milepost 418.8.

**Falls at Yellowstone Prong at Graveyard Fields (MP 418.8)**

The grass and heath balds that dominate a number of southern Appalachian summits can be found along the Blue Ridge Parkway at Craggy Gardens (milepost 364.5) and at Old Bald (milepost 434.2). Grassy balds are usually covered with grasses, sedges, and other low-growing plants; heath balds are usually covered with shrubs such as rhododendrons, mountain laurels, and blueberries. Craggy Gardens supports both types of balds.

Similar in appearance to the tundra that occurs above the Arctic circle, balds differ in that the elevation is often below tree line and the summits lower than those topped by spruce and fir forests. Decades of debate have tried to answer the question, "Why are the balds treeless?" No one seems to know how long balds have existed in the southern Appalachians, but Cherokee lore mentions the existence of balds.

Theories abound: balds were cleared by European settlers or the Cherokees, ice and windstorms killed the trees on the summits, climatic changes during the past few thousand years killed the spruce and fir on some peaks, or the trees were killed by insects. There is evidence to support all these theories, as well as evidence to refute them all.

Whatever the reason, once the trees were gone, something kept them from growing back. Theories abound on this subject, too. Perhaps the thick grass prevented other plants from gaining a foothold, harsh weather conditions prevented trees from reseeding, or the continual grazing of animals (livestock, elk, deer) kept the balds clear.

Scientists do agree on one thing: the balds are disappearing. With the elimination of grazing, the balds are slowly being encroached on by the forest. Within a few decades (unless we intervene), balds in the southern Appalachians will disappear altogether.

## 418.8

### Graveyard Fields Overlook

Graveyard Fields Loop Trail (2.3-mile loop, moderate) leads to a bridge over the Yellowstone Prong of the Pigeon's east fork and provides access to Second Falls and Yellowstone Falls (turn right after bridge) and Upper Falls (turn left after bridge).

The barren landscape along the prong favors a piece of the Rocky Mountains. In 1925, a fire destroyed 25,000 acres of spruce and fir trees in Pisgah National Forest and created an open pocket of land where the remaining stumps resemble gravestones. Almost completely bald until the late 1980s, the fields are now being reclaimed by first-generation trees, in addition to shrubs such as laurels, rhododendrons, serviceberries, and honeysuckles.

## 419.4
## John Rock Overlook
John was a horse that fell off a cliff here. You can't see the cliffs of John Rock, but John Rock Trail (0.1 mile, easy) leads to views of the Davidson River Valley. Notice the network of deer trails at this overlook. A picnic table is available here.

## 420.2
## Balsam Spring Gap—FS 816/Black Balsam Road
Travel 1 mile to reach the main access point for Shining Rock Wilderness Area, 18,500 acres of mountain terrain that are accessible only by trail. Shining Rock was one of the first national wilderness areas in the East. The forest service released several pairs of eagles, which had been kept in captivity, in this wilderness area, and eagles have been spotted around Shining Rock.

## 421.2
## Art Loeb Trail Crossing
Designated a national recreational trail in 1979, this trail was named after Carolina Mountain Club member Arthur J. Loeb. At 30.1 miles, it is the longest trail in the Pisgah District. Closest parking for access is at Fetterbush Overlook (milepost 421.7).

## 421.7
## Fetterbush Overlook
The elevation and rock outcrops in the vicinity meet the needs of the fetterbush, part of the heath family that displays attractive white blossoms in early spring. The bush's name comes from its reputation for tangling and trapping hunting dogs. Parking and access for Art Loeb Trail.

## 422.1
## Devil's Courthouse Tunnel
This tunnel is 665 feet in length.

## 422.4
## View Devil's Courthouse
Devil's Courthouse Trail (0.4 miles, strenuous) climbs through a spruce-fir forest to the 5,462-foot summit of Devil's Courthouse. The 360-degree view encompasses three states: South Carolina, Georgia, and Tennessee. A metal, compasslike plaque pinpoints mountains on the horizon. According to Cherokee belief, the Devil had a courtroom in a cave inside this mountain where he

delivered judgment to those who went astray. To avoid damaging rare plants, please stay on the trail.

This is the southernmost spot on the Parkway to watch the annual hawk migration.

### 422.8
### View Mount Hardy

The United Daughters of the Confederacy put a plaque on this mountain in 1942 as a memorial to 125,000 North Carolina veterans of the Civil War, and they planted trees in memory of Confederate soldier and physician Dr. James Hardy. The evergreens they planted now obscure any views. A picnic table is at this overlook.

### 423.2
### Beech Gap—NC 215

Canton, northwest 24 miles; 18 miles east to Rosman. Beech trees, which withstand strong winds, collect here.

### 423.4
### Courthouse Valley Overlook

Long-range views of Courthouse Valley, which joins the flatlands of the French Broad River.

### 424.4
### View Herrin Knob

The dark green of the valley below signifies local Christmas-tree farms.

### 424.8
### Wolf Mountain Overlook

Wolf Mountain is in the distance just beyond Wolf Lake—once the last stronghold of the wolf in this area. After the buffalo and the elk were extirpated, circa 1800 and 1850, respectively, the wolf, which lives primarily on large-hoofed mammals, turned to hogs and sheep for food. The last remaining wolves were shot by farmers by the early 1900s. Today, wolves have been reintroduced in Great Smoky Mountains National Park.

### 425.4
### View Rough Butt Bald

Butt describes the place where a mountain breaks off and creates a cliff. View a jagged rock outcrop beyond the sign.

### 427.6
### Bear Pen Gap Parking Area

The first of several overlooks commemorating the area's

large population of black bears. The number of bears along this stretch has declined recently due to poachers.

### 427.8
### Spot Knob Overlook
Elevation 5,652 feet.

### 428.1
### Caney Fork Overlook
Wide-range views.

### 428.9
### Bear Trap Gap
Early hunters used two- to three-foot traps to catch bears; this gap is one of many the bears often traveled through. This area is part of the 32,175-acre Pisgah Bear Sanctuary. Find a picnic table and exhibit on black bears here.

### 430.4
### Beartrail Ridge Parking Area
This overlook was named for bear trails that crisscross this area. A picnic table is at this parking area.

### 430.7
### Cowee Mountain Overlook
Here, you will find the classic ridge after ridge scene overlooking the Cowee Mountain range.

View from Cowee Mountain Overlook (MP 430.7)

Springhouses are a common sight along the Parkway. They can be found at a number of sites, including the Humpback Rocks Mountain Farm Museum at milepost 5.8, the Johnson Farm at milepost 85.9, Brinegar Cabin at milepost 238.5, and Buck Springs Lodge at milepost 407.6.

The springhouse was the settler's walk-in refrigerator. A shelter of stone was built over the spring, whose cold water welling up from the ground kept milk, butter, eggs, and other food items cool and fresh.

### 431.0

### Haywood-Jackson Overlook

This overlook was named for the junction of Haywood and Jackson counties. Richland Balsam Self-Guiding Trail (1.5-mile loop, moderate) allows you to witness the balsam woolly adelgid's attack on Fraser firs. A picnic table is here.

### 431.4

### Richland Balsam Overlook

This is the highest point on the Parkway. The overlook elevation is 6,047 feet. Look across the motor road to view Richland Balsam Mountain, elevation 6,410 feet. To reach the summit, hike Richland Balsam Trail from Haywood-Jackson Overlook (milepost 431.0).

### 432.6

### Lone Bald Overlook

Named for the last standing red spruce, or he-balsam, that once stood on this mountain.

### 433.3

### Roy Taylor Forest Overlook

A short walkway (100 feet) leads to a pedestrian over-look. An octagon-shaped deck offers a look at reforesta-tion. Interpretive plaques tell the story of the Roy Taylor Forest, designated to call attention to a congressman's efforts to safeguard our natural resources.

### 435.1

### View Doubletop Mountain

This parking area is located in Flat Gap, which was used by loggers and hunters as a campsite in the 1800s. Below is Deep Ridge Creek, the site of a Cherokee village until 1781, when it was destroyed because the Cherokee were allied to the British. A picnic table is here.

**435.7**
**Licklog Gap Overlook**
Settlers drove their cattle to high ground in the summer. Here, in a gap, they "salted" them, placing salt for the animals in hollowed-out logs. A picnic table is here.

**436.8**
**Grassy Ridge Mine Overlook**
Below, a mica mine existed prior to the Civil War. A picnic table is at this overlook.

**438.9**
**View Steestachee Bald**
*Steestachee* is the Cherokee word for "mouse."

**439.3**
**Cove Field Ridge Overlook**
Elevation 4,620 feet; long-range views.

**439.7**
**Pinnacle Ridge Tunnel**
The Parkway's second-longest tunnel at 813 feet.

**440.0**
**View Village of Saunook**
View of Saunook, a small community near Waynesville.

**440.9**
**View Waynesville**
Winter views of Waynesville, which lies below Plott Balsam Range. Legend says the town was named for Revolutionary War hero "Mad" Anthony Wayne. A picnic table is here.

**441.3**
**Standing Rock Overlook**
Named for the large, standing rock on the southern edge of the parking area. A picnic table is located here.

**441.9**
**Rabb Knob Overlook**
In 1776 General Griffith Rutherford led an attack that pushed Native Americans living along the Tuckasegee River back into what is now Cherokee and destroyed their cabins.

**442.3**
**Balsam Gap Overlook**
This parking area with a picnic table is named for the balsams seen here.

**443.1**

**Balsam Gap—US 74/23**

Eight miles to Waynesville; 12 miles to Sylva.

**444.4**

**The Orchards**

This parking area with picnic table is on a short loop off the Parkway. It is named for the apple orchards alongside Richland Creek in the valley below.

**445.2**

**View Mount Lynn Lowry**

The 60-foot cross on the mountaintop honors General Sumter Lowry's daughter, who died of leukemia in 1962. Six lights constantly burn in her memory. In winter, view Woodfin Cascades across the valley. A picnic table is here.

**446.7**

**Woodfin Cascades Overlook**

You can hear the waterfalls, but Woodfin Cascades must be viewed from milepost 445.2 during winter.

**447.8**

**View Wesner Bald**

Elevation 4,914 feet.

**448.2**

**Scott Creek**

Elevation 5,050 feet.

**449.0**

**Fork Ridge Overlook**

This overlook is literally a mile high.

**450.2**

**View Yellow Face**

A Black Rock Lumber Company logging camp, once situated nearby, floated logs off the mountain to Sylva using a flume and diverted creek water. In winter, when the moss on the mountain died, the rock face appeared yellow.

**451.2**

**Waterrock Knob Overlook**

The Plott Balsam Range and the Great Balsam Range meet at Waterrock Knob, the second-highest point on the Parkway. Display boards point out prominent peaks on the horizon, adding distances and explanation of names. Because the parking area offers views to the southwest and the northeast, this spot is ideal for watching the sunrise and sunset. Waterrock Knob Trail (1.2 miles, strenuous) ends at the summit of Waterrock Knob. With an elevation of 6,400 feet, this trail goes higher than any other trail along the Parkway. A visitor center and interpretive area at this lofty vantage point introduce visitors to black bears, endangered firs, and other natural and cultural aspects of this rugged terrain.

On your way up the spur road to the large parking area, stop at the overlook named View Browning Knob and read the plaque in honor of engineer R. Getty Browning. He played a big part in the present-day location of the Parkway through North Carolina. Picnic tables and pit-style toilets are also available at this parking area.

### 452.1
### View Cranberry Ridge
The ridge is 900 feet below this overlook. Mountain cranberry is a shrub rather than a vine (like those grown in bogs in the northeast). In late summer their brightly colored berries attract large numbers of native birds.

### 452.3
### Woolyback Overlook
Woolyback refers to the thicket created by mountain laurels and rhododendrons so dense that you could almost walk on it.

### 453.4
### View Hornbuckle Valley
This valley was the stage for an 1864 Civil War battle in which the Cherokee wore Confederate gray and kept the Union from taking their land. Ironically, the valley was named for James Hornbuckle, a Cherokee who farmed the area and served in the Union army.

### 454.3
### Thunder Struck Ridge
The ridge can be seen 100 feet below.

### 455.1
### Fed Cove Overlook
A man named Fed once owned a cabin in the cove below. He coexisted peacefully with the Cherokee, particularly noteworthy as the area was turbulent during the Civil War.

### 455.7
### Soco Gap—US 19/Overlook

Follow US 19 0.4 miles north to Maggie Valley, 12 miles south to Cherokee. Soco Creek and Gap are from the mispronunciation of the Cherokee word *Sa-gwa-hi*, "one place." For the Cherokee this gap was ahaluna, or "place of ambush," named for a Cherokee ambush that killed all but one of a large invading party of Shawnees. The survivor's ear was cut off, and he was sent back to his tribe as a warning. This gap was the initial point of the 1876 U.S. Survey for the Cherokee Indian Reservation.

### 456.2
### Jonathan Creek

This creek was named for pioneer Jonathan MacPeters.

### 457.9
### View Plott Balsam

The Plott Balsam Mountains, the southernmost range that the Parkway crosses, was home to the prized Plott hounds. In the early 1800s, Amos Plott and his family developed a dog tenacious enough to hunt bear. These Plott hounds were descended from hunting dogs that Amos's grandfather, Johannes, brought to America from his native Germany. Waterrock Knob is also known as Amos Plott Balsam. One tale recounts how Plott's hunting dogs cornered a bear in a hole. Amos took after the bear with a knife. The struggle ended with the bear dead and Amos badly bleeding. He recovered from his wounds but was never again known to go after a bear with a knife.

### 458.2
### Wolf Laurel Gap—Heintooga Spur Road

A 9-mile spur road accessing the southeastern corner of the Great Smoky Mountains National Park.

### 0.9

Mollie Gap and Indian Road accesses Soco Bald.

### 1.3

Mile High Overlook provides information on Great Smoky Mountains National Park.

### 1.4

Maggie Valley Overlook offers a view of the lights in Maggie Valley during the winter.

**3.6**

Black Camp Gap has a paved walk to a historic Masonic marker. The gap was named for people who were often covered in ash because the walls of the cabin where they lived had been charred by fire.

**4.8**

View Flat Creek Falls in the winter.

**6.0**

Paul's Gap accesses several trails leading into the Great Smoky Mountains National Park.

**8.4**

Balsam Mountain Campground.

**8.9**

Heintooga Ridge Picnic Area.

**9.0**

Pavement ends at gated, gravel Round Bottom Road.

**458.8**
### Lickstone Ridge Tunnel
A lick stone, like a lick-log, was a salt lick for animals. This tunnel is 402 feet.

**458.9**
### Lickstone Ridge Overlook
Below, the Cherokee Reservation (Qualla Boundary) can be traced to a band of Cherokee who took refuge in the Smokies when their tribe was forcibly removed to Oklahoma in 1838.

**459.3**
### Bunches Bald Tunnel
One of the shortest tunnels on the Parkway at 255 feet.

**459.4**
### Bunches Bald Overlook
This parking area is located at the south end of the tunnel. The bald was likely named after an early logger.

**460.7**
### Jenkins Ridge Overlook
The ridge was named for Jonas Jenkins, an early settler who coexisted on amicable terms with the Cherokee and

lived on the far side of the ridge visible to the left.

## 461.2
### Big Witch Tunnel
This tunnel is 348 feet.

## 461.9
### Big Witch Overlook
Named for one of the last great Cherokee medicine men, the overlook offers picnic tables along with good views of the Smoky Mountains.

## 463.9
### View Thomas Divide
Thomas Divide is near Bryson City, North Carolina.

## 465.6
### Rattlesnake Mountain Tunnel
This tunnel is 395 feet long.

## 466.2
### Sherrill Cove Tunnel
The tunnel is 550 feet in length.

## 467.4
### View Ballhoot Scar
Ballhoot, a logging term, refers to the method of skidding logs off the mountain at steep places on the hillside, which leaves a slick scar behind.

## 467.9
### View Raven Fork
The fields below, Floyd Bottoms, are in the Great Smoky Mountains National Park.

## 468.4
### View Oconaluftee River
*Oconaluftee*, a Cherokee word, means "beside the river."

## 469.0
### Oconaluftee River Bridge

## 469.1
### US 441
The southern terminus of the Blue Ridge Parkway. Gatlinburg lies 29 miles west (traveling through the Great Smoky Mountains National Park); drive 2 miles south to Cherokee.

# Blue Ridge Parkway Bloom Calendar

• • • • • • • • • • • • • • •

**Skunk Cabbage** *Symplocarpus foetidus*   Feb–Mar
176.1, 185.8, 217

**Dandelion** *Taraxacum officinale*   Feb–June
Common along roadside

**Dwarf Iris** *Iris verna*   Mar–Apr
260.5

**Mayapple** *Podophyllum peltatum*
76.2–76.4, 296–297, 315–317, 320.8, 339.5

**Spring Beauty** *Claytonia caroliniana*
367.6

**Bird's-foot Violet** *Viola pedata*   Mar–May
147.4, 202, 260.5, 379

**Serviceberry or Sarvis** *Amelanchier arborea*
241–242, 294–297, 308.3, 347.6, 368–370

**Silverbell Tree** *Halesia carolina*
344.1–355.3

**Buttercups** *Ranunculus hispidus*   Mar–Jun
Common along roadside

**Wild Strawberry** *Fragaria virginiana*
Common along roadside

Field mouse

**Solomon's Seal** *Polygonatum biflorum*
Common on moist wooded slopes and coves

Apr–May

**Squirrel Corn** *Dicentra canadensis*
367.6, 458.2 and along Heintooga Spur Road

**Trillium** *Trillium spp.*
175, 200–216, 339–340, 364.6

**Tulip Poplar** *Liriodendron tulipifera*
Common in low woods and coves

**Fetterbush** *Leucothoe racemosa*
241.1, 379

late Apr–May

**Redbud** *Cercia canadensis*
54–68

**Black Locust** *Robinia pseudo-acacia*
100–123, 367–368, 383

Apr–June

**Dutchman's Breeches** *Dicentra cucullaria*
67.6, 458.2 and along Heintooga Spur Road

**False Solomon's Seal** *Smilacina racemosa*
Common along roadside

**Foam Flower** *Tiarella cordifolia*
296.9, 339.5, 367.7

**Witch-Hobble or Hobblebush** *Viburnum alniflorum*
Aug. (fruit): 295.5, 362–367, higher elevations in
rich, moist woods

**Carolina Rhododendron** *Rhododendron minus*
308–310, 404–411

late Apr–June

**Heal All** *Prunella vulgaris*
Common along roadside

Apr–first frost

**Dogwood** *Cornus florida*
6, 85.8, 154.5, 230–232, 217–219, 378–382

May

**Fraser Magnolia** *Magnolia fraseri*
173–174, 252–253

**Large Flowered Trillium** *Trillium grandiflorum*
3–7, 64–85, 154.5, 168–169, 175, 330–340, 370–375

**Allegheny Blackberry** *Rubus allegheniensis*
6, 167.2, 239.9, 305–315, 339.5, 367.6

May–June

**Bluets** *Houstonia spp.*
200.2, 355–368

**Bead Lily** *Clintonia umbellulata*
Common in rich, moist deciduous woods

**Bittersweet** *Celastrus orbiculatus*
Aug.–Sept. (berry): 242.4, 383, 394, 396

**Bowman's Root** *Gillenia trifoliata*
24–25, 149.5, 260, 332, 368–369

**Bristly Locust** *Robinia hispida*
167–174, 308.3, 347.9

**Field Hawkweed** *Hieracium pratense*
6, 78.4, 165.5, 229.5, 325–330

| May–June | **Fire Pink** *Silene virginica* |
| | 1–2, 85.8, 154.5, 241, 339.3, 367–375, 404–408 |
| | **Flame Azalea** *Rhododendron calendulaceum* |
| | 138.6, 144–145, 149.5, 164–166, 217–221, 308–310, 368–380, 412–423 |
| | **Hawthorne** *Crataegus spp.* |
| | 155–176, 365.6, 368 |
| | **New Jersey Tea** *Ceanothus americanus* |
| | 42–43, 91–100, 138.4, 197, 211, 241, 328.6 |
| | **Pinkshell Azalea** *Rhododendron vaseyi* |
| | 305.2, 342–343, 349–351, 419–424 |
| | **Red Berried Elder** *Sambucus pubens* |
| | 355–360, 369, 412–425, higher elevations in rich, moist woods |
| | **Small's Groundsel** *Senecio smallii* |
| | 29.1, 85.8, 330–340 |
| | **Staghorn Sumac** *Rhus typhina* |
| | Common along roadside in dry, rocky areas |
| | **Wild Geranium** *Geranium maculatum* |
| | 84–86, 170–172, 211.6, 375 |
| May–July | **Columbine** *Aquilegia canadensis* |
| | 74–75, 339.3, 370–378 |
| | **Fly Poison** *Amianthium muscaetoxicum* |
| | 210–216, 406–408 |
| | **Galax** *Galax aphylla* |
| | Common in deciduous forest and open rocky areas |
| | **Phlox** *Phlox carolina* |
| | 4, 79–82, 163–164, 200–202, 219–221, 339.3, 370–380 |
| May–Aug | **Bladder Campion** *Silene cucubalus* |
| | 376–381 |
| May–Sept | **Queen Anne's Lace** *Daucus carota* |
| | Common in open fields and along roadside |
| late May–June | **Mountain Laurel** *Kalmia latifolia* |
| | 130.5, 162.9, 347.9, 380, 400 |
| late May–July | **Virginia Spiderwort** *Tradescantia subaspera* |
| | 85.8 and along Sharp Top Trail, 380–381 |
| June | **Goat's Beard** *Aruncus dioicus* |
| | 10–11, 24, 240, 337.6, 370–375 |
| | **Sundrops** *Oenothera fruticosa* |
| | 8–10, 89–91, 229, 270.6, 351–352, 355–360, 370–375 |
| | **Tree of Heaven** *Ailanthus altissima* |
| | 382, common along roadside in Virginia |
| | **Viper's Bugloss** *Echium vulgare* |
| | 5–40 |
| June–early July | **Catawba Rhododendron** *Rhododenron catawbiense* |
| | 44.9, 77–83, 130.5, 138.6, 239, 247, 266.8, 348–350, 364.1 |

American Elder *Sambucus canadensis*  June–July
29, 85.8, 136–138, 272–275, 311.2

Beardtongue *Penstemon spp.*
44.4, 89–91, 154.5, 254.5, 339–340, 370–372

Fragrant Thimbleberry *Rubus odoratus*
18, 74.7, 339.3, 369–372, 406–408

Mountain Ash *Sorbus americana*
Sept.–Oct. (berry): Mt. Mitchell and Mt. Pisgah,
higher spruce-fir forests

Sourwood *Oxydendrum arboreum*
102–106, 231–232, 321–327, 375–380

Spiraea *Spiraea japonica*
368–378

White Rhododendron *Rhododendron maximum*
162.9, 169, 232–233, 339.3, 352–353, 455–456

Butter and Eggs *Linaria vulgaris*  June–Aug
Common along roadside

Butterfly Weed *Asclepias tuberosa*
63–65, 238–246

Coreopsis *Coreopsis pubescens*
29.6, 77, 157, 190, 306

Deptford Pink *Dianthus armeria*
Common along grassy roadside

False Hellebore *Veratrum viride*
364.6 and along Craggy Gardens trails

Turkscap Lily *Lilium superbum*
187.6, 364–368, 406–411

Mullein *Verbascum thapsus*  June–Sept
Common along roadside on dry banks

Bull Thistle *Carduus lanceolatus*  late June–first frost
Common along roadside

Black Cohosh *Cimicifuga recemosa*  July
6, 85.8, 169, 374

Black-Eyed Susan *Rudbeckia hirta*
Common in fields and along roadside

Fleabane *Erigeron Strigosus*
Common in fields and along roadside

Ox-Eye Daisy *Chrysanthemum leucanthemum*
Common in fields and along roadside

Tall Meadow Rue *Thalictrum polygamum*
85.8, 155.2, 248

Yarrow *Achillea millefolium*
Common in fields and along roadside

Bergamot Bee Balm *Monarda fistulosa*  July–Aug
38.8, 368–374

| | |
|---|---|
| July–Aug | **Common Milkweed** *Asclepias syriaca* |
| | 85–86, 167–176 |
| | **Oswego Tea** *Monarda didyma* |
| | Common in wet areas at higher elevations |
| | **Tall Coneflower** *Rudbeckia laciniata* |
| | 36, 161.2, 228.1, 314, 359–368 |
| July–Sept | **Bellflower** *Campanula americana* |
| | 370–375 |
| | **Starry Campion** *Silene stellata* |
| | 378–380 |
| July–Oct | **White Snakeroot** *Eupatorium rugosum* |
| | Common along roadside |
| Aug | **Boneset** *Eupatorium perfoliatum* |
| | 29.1, 85.8, 151, 247, 314 |
| | **Cardinal Flower** *Lobelia cardinalis* |
| | Infrequently in wet areas |
| | **Ironweed** *Venonia noveboracensis* |
| | 245, 248 |
| | **Jewelweed or Touch-Me-Not** *Impatiens capensis* |
| | Common along roadside in wet areas |
| | **Joe-Pye Weed** *Eupatorium purpureum* |
| | 6, 85.8, 146, 248, 339.3, 357–359 |
| | **Pokeberry** *Phytolacca americana* |
| | 6, 74.7, 151, 239.9, 323, 376.9 |
| | **Virgins Bower** *Clematis virginia* |
| | 85.8, 131.1, 176.1, 285–289, 313–314 |
| Aug–Sept | **Angelica** *Anegelica triquinata* |
| | 294.7, 339.5, 355, 367.6 along Craggy Gardens trails |
| | **Blazing Star** *Liatris spicata* |
| | 305.1, 369–370 |
| | **Dodder or Love Vine** *Cuscuta rostrata* |
| | Common along roadside |
| | **Sneezeweed** *Helenium autumnale* |
| | 29.1, 85.8, 176.1, 229, 313–314 |
| Aug–first frost | **Nodding Ladies' Tresses** *Spiranthes cernua* |
| | 365–368 |
| late Aug–first frost | **Gentian** *Gentiana quinquefolia* |
| | 85.8, 363–368 |
| Sept | **Aster** *Aster spp.* |
| | Common in fields and along roadside |
| | **Goldenrod** *Solidago spp.* |
| | Common in fields and along roadside |
| Sept–Oct | **Yellow Ironweed** *Actinomeris alternifolia* |
| | 6, 88, 154.5, 271.9, 330.8 |
| late Sept–Oct | **Witch Hazel** *Hamamelis virginiana* |
| | 130.5, 293.3, 295.4, 305.1, 308.3, 339.5, 347.6, 367.7 |

# Blue Ridge Parkway Contact Information

• • • • • • • • • • • • • • • • • • • • •

## General Information Numbers

| | |
|---|---|
| Blue Ridge Parkway (Campgrounds) | (877) 444-6777 |
| www.recreation.gov | |
| Blue Ridge Parkway (Emergency) | (800) 727-5928 |
| Blue Ridge Parkway (Headquarters) | (828) 271-4779 |
| Blue Ridge Parkway (Information) | (828) 298 0398 |
| www.nps.gov/blri | |
| Blue Ridge Parkway Association | www.blueridgeparkway.org |
| Blue Ridge Parkway Foundation | (336) 721-0260 |
| www.brpfoundation.org | |
| Conservation Trust for North Carolina | (919) 828-4199 |
| www.ctnc.org | |
| Eastern National | (828) 298-2774 |
| www.easternnational.org | |
| Friends of the Blue Ridge Parkway | (800) 228-7275 |
| www.blueridgefriends.org | |
| George Washington and Jefferson national forests | |
| www.southernregion.fs.fed.us/gwj | (540) 265-5100 |
| Great Smoky Mountains National Park | (865) 436-1200 |
| www.nps.gov/grsm | |
| Nantahala National Forest | (828) 257-4200 |
| www.cs.unca.edu/nfsnc | |
| National Council for the Traditional Arts | (301) 565-0654 |
| www.ncta.net | |
| Pisgah National Forest | (828) 257-4200 |
| www.cs.unca.edu/nfsnc | |
| Shenandoah National Park | (540) 999-3500 |
| www.nps.gov/shen | |
| Southern Highland Craft Guild | (828) 298-7928 |
| www.southernhighlandguild.org | |

## Important Contacts along the Parkway

| | | |
|---|---|---|
| 5.8 | Humpback Rocks Visitor Center | (540) 943-4716 |
| 60.8 | Otter Creek Restaurant | (434) 299-5862 |
| 63.6 | James River Visitor Center | (434) 299-5496 |
| 85.6 | Peaks of Otter Lodge | (540) 586-1081 or |
| | www.peaksofotter.com | (800) 542-5927 |
| 85.9 | Peaks of Otter Visitor Center | (540) 586-4496 |
| 85.9 | Peaks of Otter Camp Store | (540) 586-1614 |
| 115.0 | Virginia's Explore Park | (540) 772-2010 |
| | www.explorepark.org | |
| 169.0 | Rocky Knob Visitor Center | (540) 745-9662 |
| 174.1 | Rocky Knob Hskpg. Cabins | (540) 593-3503 |
| | www.blueridgeresort.com | |
| 176.2 | Mabry Mill Restaurant & Gifts | (276) 952-2947 |

Fall flowers          **\* Indicates exit to take brief drive off of Parkway**

# Trailheads on the Blue Ridge Parkway

## VIRGINIA

| Milepost | Trail | Length | Difficulty |
|---|---|---|---|
| 5.9 | Mountain Farm Trail | 0.25 | Easy |
| 6.0 | Appalachian Trail | 2.0 | Strenuous |
| 8.4 | Catoctin Loop Trail | 0.3 | Moderate |
| 8.8 | Greenstone Trail | 0.2 | Moderate |
| 17.6 | Priest Overlook Trail | 0.2 | Easy |
| 18.5 | White Rock Falls Trail Conn. | 2.9 | Moderate |
| 20.0 | White Rock Falls Trail | 0.9 | Moderate |
| 26.3 | Big Spy Trail | 0.1 | Moderate |
| 29.0 | Whetstone Ridge Trail | 12.0 | Mod./Stren. |
| 34.4 | Yankee Horse Trail | 0.2 | Moderate |
| 38.8 | Boston Knob LoopTrail | 0.1 | Easy |
| 47.5 | Indian Gap Trail | 0.2 | Moderate |
| 55.2 | White Oak Flats Trail | 0.1 | Easy |
| 60.8 | Otter Creek Trail | 3.5 | Moderate |
| 63.1 | Otter Lake Loop Trail | 0.8 | Moderate |
| 63.6 | James River Canal Trail | 0.2 | Easy |
| 63.6 | Trail of Trees Trail | 0.5 | Moderate |
| 74.7 | Thunder Ridge Trail | 0.1 | Easy |
| 78.4 | Apple Orchard Falls Trail | 1.2 | Strenuous |
| 79.7 | Onion Mountain Loop Trail | 0.2 | Easy |
| 83.1 | Falling Water Cascades Trail | 1.6 | Moderate |
| 83.5 | Flat Top Trail | 4.4 | Moderate |
| 85.7 | Abbott Lake Trail | 1.0 | Easy |
| 85.9 | Elk Run Loop Trail | 0.8 | Easy |
| 85.9 | Johnson Farm Loop Trail | 2.1 | Moderate |
| 85.9 | Harkening Hill Loop Trail | 3.3 | Moderate |
| 86.0 | Sharp Top Trail | 3.2 | Strenuous |
| 91.0 | Appalachian Trail | 1.9 | Moderate |
| 92.5 | Appalachian Trail | 2.9 | Moderate |
| 95.4 | Appalachian Trail | 0.6 | Moderate |
| 95.9 | Appalachian Trail | 1.0 | Moderate |
| 96.0 | Spec Mine Trail | 2.8 | Strenuous |
| 97.0 | Appalachian Trail | 0.8 | Moderate |
| 110.6 | Stewarts Knob Trail | 0.1 | Easy |
| 114.9 | Roanoke River Trail | 0.4 | Easy |
| 120.4 | Roanoke Mtn. Summit Trail | 0.11 | Moderate |
| 120.5 | Chestnut Ridge Trail | 5.4 | Moderate |
| 121.4 | Roanoke Valley Horse Trail | 18.5 | Moderate |
| 123.2 | Buck Mountain Trail | 0.53 | Moderate |
| 154.5 | Smart View Loop Trail | 2.6 | Moderate |

## VIRGINIA (continued)

| Milepost | Trail | Length | Difficulty |
|---|---|---|---|
| 167.1 | Rock Castle Gorge Trail | 10.8 | Strenuous |
| 167.1 | Hardwood Cove Nature Trail | 0.8 | Moderate |
| 169.0 | Black Ridge Trail | 3.1 | Moderate |
| 169.0 | Rocky Knob Picnic Area Loop | 1.0 | Easy |
| 176.2 | Mountain Industry Trail | 1.0 | Easy |
| 179.2 | Round Meadow Creek Loop | 0.5 | Moderate |

## NORTH CAROLINA

| Milepost | Trail | Length | Difficulty |
|---|---|---|---|
| 213.3 | Fisher Peak Loop Trail | 2.24 | Moderate |
| 213.3 | High Meadow Trail | 2.7 | Easy |
| 217.5 | Cumberland Knob Trail | 0.5 | Easy |
| 217.5 | Gully Creek Trail | 2.0 | Strenuous |
| 218.6 | Fox Hunters Paradise Trail | 0.2 | Easy |
| 230.1 | Little Glade Mill Pond | 0.3 | Easy |
| 238.5 | Bluff Mountain Trail | 7.5 | Moderate |
| 238.5 | Cedar Ridge Trail | 4.3 | Moderate |
| 241.0 | Bluff Ridge Primitive Trail | 2.89 | Strenuous |
| 241.0 | Fodder Stack Trail | 1.0 | Moderate |
| 243.7 | Basin Creek Trail | 3.3 | Moderate |
| 243.7 | Grassy Gap Fire Road | 6.5 | Moderate |
| 244.7 | Flat Rock Ridge Trail | 5.0 | Moderate |
| 260.3 | Jumpinoff Rocks Trail | 1.0 | Easy |
| 264.4 | Lump Trail | 0.3 | Easy |
| 271.9 | Cascades Trail | 0.6 | Moderate |
| 272.5 | Tompkins Knob Trail | 0.5 | Easy |
| 294.0 | Bass Lake Road | 1.0 | Easy |
| 294.0 | Black Bottom Road | 0.5 | Easy |
| 294.0 | Deer Park Road | 0.8 | Moderate |
| 294.0 | Duncan Road | 2.5 | Moderate |
| 294.0 | Flat Top Mountain Trail | 3.0 | Moderate |
| 294.0 | Maze Trail | 2.3 | Moderate |
| 294.0 | Rich Mountain Trail | 4.3 | Moderate |
| 294.0 | Rock Creek Bridge Trail | 1.0 | Easy |
| 294.0 | Watkin Road | 3.3 | Easy/Mod. |
| 294.1 | Figure 8 Trail | 0.7 | Easy |
| 294.6 | Trout Lake Trail | 1.0 | Easy |
| 295.9 | Green Knob Trail | 2.3 | Mod./Stren. |
| 296.5 | Boone Fork Trail | 4.9 | Mod./Stren. |
| 297.0 | Price Lake Loop Trail | 2.3 | Moderate |
| 304.4 | Linn Cove Viaduct Ac. Trail | 0.16 | Easy |
| 305.2 | Beacon Heights Trail | 0.22 | Moderate |
| 305.5 | Tanawha Trail | 13.5 | Easy/Mod. |
| 308.2 | Flat Rock Trail | 0.63 | Easy |
| 315.5 | Camp Creek Trail | 0.1 | Easy |
| 316.4 | Duggers Creek Trail | 0.3 | Easy |
| 316.4 | Linville Falls Trail | 0.8 | Moderate |
| 316.4 | Linville Gorge Trail | 0.5 | Strenuous |
| 316.5 | Linville River Bridge Trail | 0.1 | Easy |
| 320.8 | Chestoa View Trail | 0.63 | Easy |

| Milepost | Trail | Length | Difficulty |
|---|---|---|---|
| 339.5 | Crabtree Falls Loop Trail | 2.5 | Strenuous |
| 344.1 | Woods Mountain Trail | 2.0 | Moderate |
| 350.4 | Lost Cove Ridge Trail | 0.6/3.1 | Moderate |
| 351.9 | Deep Gap Trail | 0.2 | Easy |
| 355.0 | Bald Knob Ridge Trail | 2.8 | Easy |
| 359.8 | Big Butt Trail | 6.0 | Strenuous |
| 361.2 | Glassmine Falls | 0.1 | Moderate |
| 364.2 | Craggy Gardens Trail | 0.84 | Moderate |
| 364.2 | Craggy Pinnacle Trail | 1.46 | Moderate |
| 374.4 | Rattlesnake Lodge Trail | 0.5 | Moderate |
| 382.0 | MST Trail | 7.5 | Moderate |
| 393.7 | Shut-In Trail/MST Trail | 3.1 | Strenuous |
| 396.4 | Shut-In Trail/MST Trail | 1.7 | Moderate |
| 397.3 | Grassy Knob Trail | 0.9 | Strenuous |
| 397.3 | Shut-In Trail/MST Trail | 0.7 | Moderate |
| 398.3 | Shut-In Trail/MST Trail | 2.8 | Strenuous |
| 400.3 | Shut-In Trail/MST Trail | 1.9 | Moderate |
| 401.7 | Shut-In Trail/MST Trail | 0.9 | Moderate |
| 402.6 | Shut-In Trail/MST Trail | 1.2 | Strenuous |
| 403.6 | Shut-In Trail/MST Trail | 1.2 | Mod./Stren. |
| 404.5 | Shut-In Trail/MST Trail | 1.2 | Strenuous |
| 405.5 | Shut-In Trail/MST Trail | 1.7 | Strenuous |
| 407.6 | Buck Springs Trail | 1.06 | Easy/Mod. |
| 407.6 | Mt. Pisgah Trail | 1.5 | Mod./Stren. |
| 407.8 | Picnic Area Loop Trail | 0.3 | Easy |
| 408.5 | Frying Pan Mountain Trail | 1.65 | Mod./Stren. |
| 417.0 | East Fork Trail | 0.1 | Easy/Mod. |
| 418.8 | Graveyard Fields Loop Trail | 2.29 | Moderate |
| 419.4 | John Rock Trail | 0.1 | Easy |
| 421.2 | Art Loeb Trail | 30.1 | Strenuous |
| 422.4 | Devil's Courthouse Trail | 0.42 | Mod./Stren. |
| 427.6 | Bear Pen Gap Trail | 0.22 | Easy |
| 431.0 | Richland Balsam Trail | 1.47 | Moderate |
| 433.8 | Roy Taylor Overlook Trail | 0.1 | Easy |
| 451.2 | Waterrock Knob Trail | 1.18 | Mod./Stren. |

# Milepost Tunnel Guide

| Milepost | Tunnel | Length |
|---|---|---|
| 53.1 | Bluff Mountain Tunnel | 630 feet |
| 333.4 | Little Switzerland Tunnel | 542 feet |
| 336.8 | Wildacres Tunnel | 330 feet |
| 344.4 | Twin Tunnel (North) | 300 feet |
| 344.7 | Twin Tunnel (South) | 401 feet |
| 349.0 | Rough Ridge Tunnel | 150 feet |
| 364.4 | Craggy Pinnacle Tunnel | 245 feet |
| 365.5 | Craggy Flats Tunnel | 400 feet |
| 374.4 | Tanbark Ridge Tunnel | 780 feet |
| 397.1 | Grassy Knob Tunnel | 770 feet |
| 399.1 | Pine Mountain Tunnel | 1,434 feet |
| 400.9 | Ferrin Knob Tunnel #1 | 561 feet |
| 401.3 | Ferrin Knob Tunnel #2 | 421 feet |
| 401.5 | Ferrin Knob Tunnel #3 | 375 feet |
| 403.0 | Young Pisgah Ridge Tunnel | 412 feet |
| 404.0 | Fork Mountain Tunnel | 389 feet |
| 406.9 | Little Pisgah Tunnel | 576 feet |
| 407.3 | Buck Springs Tunnel | 462 feet |
| 410.1 | Frying Pan Tunnel | 577 feet |
| 422.1 | Devil's Courthouse Tunnel | 665 feet |
| 439.7 | Pinnacle Ridge Tunnel | 813 feet |
| 458.8 | Lickstone Ridge Tunnel | 402 feet |
| 459.3 | Bunches Bald Tunnel | 255 feet |
| 461.2 | Big Witch Tunnel | 348 feet |
| 465.6 | Rattlesnake Mountain Tunnel | 395 feet |
| 466.2 | Sherrill Cove Tunnel | 550 feet |

Eastern National is a private nonprofit partner of the National Park Service. Its mission is to provide quality educational products and services in America's national parks and other public trusts. Proceeds from Eastern National retail sales outlets are donated to support publications such as this one, as well as park activities in education, conservation, and research.

Look for Eastern National stores in every Parkway visitor center. Each store is uniquely focused on the local features that make the area special. The National Park Service and Eastern National have carefully selected products that will extend and enrich the quality of your park visit, as well as the memories that accompany you home.

For more information about products relating to the Blue Ridge Parkway, contact the Blue Ridge Parkway Association at (828) 299-3507, or check out its online store at www.eparks.com. Or contact the Blue Ridge Parkway Foundation at (828) 265-4026 or www. blueridgeparkwaystore.com.

The Southern Highland
Craft Guild at Moses H.
Cone Memorial Park
(MP 294.0)